BLOOMERS AND BUGLES

Other Books by ARCH MERRILL

A RIVER RAMBLE

THE LAKES COUNTRY

THE RIDGE

THE TOWPATH

ROCHESTER SKETCH BOOK

STAGECOACH TOWNS

TOMAHAWKS AND OLD LACE

LAND OF THE SENECAS

UPSTATE ECHOES

SLIM FINGERS BECKON

SHADOWS ON THE WALL

SOUTHERN TIER VOL. I

SOUTHERN TIER VOL. II

THE WHITE WOMAN AND HER VALLEY

OUR GOODLY HERITAGE

PIONEER PROFILES

BLOOMERS
AND
BUGLES

By *ARCH MERRILL*

974.7
m

Manufactured in 1958 by American Book–Stratford Press, Inc., 75 Varick Street, New York 13, N. Y., and distributed by Seneca Book Binding Company, 31 North Water Street, Rochester 4, N. Y.

Contents

List of Illustrations

BLOOMERS AND BUGLES

Chapter 1

The Age of Ferment

Between the passing of the York State frontier in the 1830s and the stillness at Appomattox in 1865 stretched an age of ferment.

It was a time that saw new trails blazed on many fronts, a time of vast expansion, of the coming of the Age of Steam, of new inventions and new machinery, of the gathering rift between the sections that erupted into civil war—and above all, the burgeoning of revolutionary new ideas in a mobile society.

In this exciting national drama a remarkable array of Central-Western New York men and women played no small parts. Most of them were daring individualists, unafraid of innovations.

The first wearing of the Bloomer costume on the streets of Seneca Falls, cradle of the feminist movement, symbolized woman's revolt against the status quo and her demand for her rightful place in a changing order. The bugles of reform called "the Bloomer Girls" of suffrage fame, Elizabeth Cady Stanton, Susan B. Anthony and Amelia Bloomer, to march under other banners, too—those of abolition, temperance and reform in dress and diet. The age of ferment was the heyday of the reformers.

Elizabeth Blackwell rates a niche in history, too. For she

3

received from Geneva College the first medical degree awarded a woman anywhere.

The Underground Railroad wound its invisible way across the countryside in the days before the Civil War and, aided by Northern abolitionists, the two intrepid Negro leaders, Frederick Douglass of Rochester and Harriet Tubman of Auburn, led hundreds of their people to freedom.

The period produced such phenomena as Modern Spiritualism, born of the mysterious "rappings" in the Fox sisters' humble home, as well as phrenology, "the science of head reading," and the octagonal style of architecture, both fathered by Orson Squire Fowler, born on a Cohocton farm.

From a "water cure" on a Dansville hilltop Dr. James Caleb Jackson preached a new gospel of health, hygiene and diet, as well as producing America's first cold breakfast food.

History holds no more poignant story than that of the missionary martyrs, Dr. Marcus Whitman and his bride, Narcissa, who left the security of their native hills to preach the Word to the Indians of the Far West.

The era heard the Great Debate over slavery that ended when a Rebel shell screamed its way toward Fort Sumter. It saw the rise of the new Republican party and the passing of the Whigs. It produced such Upstate political giants as the master boss, Thurlow Weed, and his alter ego, William H. Seward; Millard Fillmore, the only native of the region to reach the White House; Henry J. Raymond, Lima-born founder of the *New York Times,* not to mention the four governors from the area in 18 years.

The war bugles called thousands from their homes to wear the Union blue on Southern battlefields and with them went Gen. James S. Wadsworth of the Genesee Valley landed gentry to die leading a charge in the Battle of the Wilderness.

It was an age of aggressive capitalism and speculation in

4

which fortunes were made and lost. Bold men of vision pioneered in the new telegraph industry—Ezra Cornell, who built the first line and founded a great university; Rochester's Hiram Sibley, who formed America's first giant monopoly and strung the wires across a continent, and the gallant Henry O'Reilly, who gambled and lost.

The Iron Horse supplanted the canal packets and the stage coaches and the new realm of the rails evolved such dynamic characters as Dean Richmond of Batavia. Two Upstate men of humble origins, Henry Wells and William G. Fargo, pioneered in the express business and the Western line they founded became part of the folklore of America.

In the new order, two booming cities rose on the banks of the Clinton Ditch, Buffalo and Rochester, overshadowing the older communities, Canandaigua, Bath and Batavia, the seats of the pioneer land companies.

The time of the pioneers who cleared the forests and lived in log cabins was over but the men and women of this Upstate land never ceased to pioneer.

It was a momentous, as well as a slightly mad and sometimes merry time—when woman wore Bloomers and adventurous souls heard the call of far-away bugles.

Chapter 2

The Bloomer Girls

One Spring day in 1851 a comely young matron appeared on the streets of Seneca Falls in a costume the like of which the villagers had never seen on land or sea.

Under a loose fitting skirt which reached below the knees, this lady wore a pair of trousers gathered at the ankles. A modest cape completed the ensemble.

It was the trousers that shocked Seneca Falls into a dither. The idea of a female wearing pants in public was just too much—even for a village not unused to unconventional females. Shorts and slacks are commonplace today but in 1851 the exposure to masculine stares of a lady's "limb," even if swathed in breeches, was downright scandalous.

The wearer of the unorthodox garb was Mrs. Elizabeth Smith Miller of Cazenovia, daughter of the wealthy, fanatical reformer, Gerrit Smith of Peterboro. She had designed it herself. It was modeled after a costume which had been worn at water cures but never exposed to public gaze.

Mrs. Miller donned it when she came to Seneca Falls to visit her cousin, Mrs. Elizabeth Cady Stanton. That 36-year-old lady, ever eager to flout convention and tradition, was delighted with her visitor's apparel and adopted it herself. In her always lucid prose, she gave her reasons:

"To see my cousin with a lamp in one hand and a baby in

the other, walk upstairs with ease and grace while, with flowing robes, I pulled myself up with difficulty, lamp and baby out of the question, readily convinced me that there was sore need of a reform in women's dress and I promptly donned a similar costume.

"I have seen galleries of beautiful paintings and statuary in the Old World but nowhere is the ideal female form to be found in a whale-boned bodice and bedraggled skirt. If the graceful is what you aim at, study the old painters and sculptors, not Godey's Book of Fashion. But for us commonplace, every day, working characters who wash and iron, bake and brew, carry water and fat babies upstairs and down, bring potatoes, apples and pans of milk from the cellar, run our own errands through mud and snow, shovel paths and work in the garden—why the 'drapery' is quite too much. One might as well work with a ball and chain. Is being born a woman so criminal an offense that we must be doomed to everlasting bondage?"

The sight of the two cousins strolling the streets of Seneca Falls in the outlandish new garb caused a buzz of excited comment that rose above the spatter of the waterfall that gave the village its name.

It remained for a lady editor who lived in Seneca Falls to spread the word of the new fashion to far places. She was Mrs. Amelia Jenks Bloomer, a 33 year old native of Homer, N.Y., and the wife of the village postmaster. Mrs. Bloomer edited a little magazine, the *Lily*, mostly devoted to her favorite cause of temperance. She described in considerable detail the new costume that had been introduced in her village. Editors all over the country picked up the item and commented on it, some with indulgent amusement, others with derisive sarcasm. It was held up as another eccentricity of that new arrival on the American scene, the "strong-minded female."

For want of a better name, the newest quirk of rebellious womanhood was dubbed the Bloomer costume after the woman who first wrote about it. Thus the name of Amelia Bloomer went into the dictionary, attached forever to a garment she did not originate, was not the first to wear and which she merely publicized.

The word, bloomer, eventually came to be identified only with the trousers part of the ensemble. The short bloomers worn in recent years by young women and girls in gymnasiums are not much like the long mannish trousers that made their debut in Seneca Falls in 1851.

After the two Elizabeths set the style, other women, all of them dedicated to temperance, anti-slavery, equal rights or other reforms, began wearing the costume of emancipation from long skirts, layers of petticoats and tight corsets. Some of the "Bloomer Girls" even had their hair cut short.

Of course, Mrs. Bloomer was an early wearer of the costume that bore her name. Lucy Stone, who pioneered in retention of her maiden name after marriage, wore the bloomers. Susan B. Anthony, a newcomer to the reform ranks, followed suit and even bobbed her hair.

The women had to endure all sorts of ridicule, written by satirical editors and shouted by urchins. The bloomers inspired such limericks as:

> *Heigh! Ho! the carrion crow,*
> *The bloomer now is all the go.*
> *Twenty tailors take the stitches;*
> *Twenty women wear the breeches.*
> *Heigh! Ho! In rain or snow,*
> *The bloomer now is all the go."*

8

Hardly more than "twenty women wore the breeches" during the four years of their vogue. Then the strong-minded female reformers, one by one, went back to long skirts. Susan B. Anthony gave one of the principal reasons for abandoning the costume:

"I found it impossible to hold a man's attention to my talk while he was completely occupied in gazing at my ankles."

Dress reform was only a side issue in the long struggle for women's rights. Still in the early years of the movement the bloomers symbolized women's desperate desire to escape from what Mrs. Stanton had called "everlasting bondage." Besides the bloomers made good propaganda for the cause.

* * *

Three years before Elizabeth Miller first wore the bloomers in Seneca Falls, that Central New York village had been the scene of the first women's rights rally in American history.

The seeds of that historic session were sown in 1840 at the world Anti-Slavery Convention in London, England. In that day women, under the old English common law, were an inferior and subject class with hardly any rights at all. In 1840 it was still the Middle Ages insofar as women were concerned. Women were to be seen but not heard. Their place was in the home, in the kitchen, in the nursery, in the connubial bed—never at a public meeting, save at church.

Nevertheless the American delegation to the London convention included some distinguished women who were active in the abolitionist movement. One was Lucretia Mott, a cultured Quakeress. In London she met young Elizabeth Cady Stanton, honeymooning with her lawyer husband, Henry B. Stanton, a delegate to the convention. The Stantons then lived in Johnstown, N.Y.

Imagine the wrath of the American women who had traveled across the ocean to attend a meeting dedicated to the end of human bondage only to see their credentials rejected and to be barred from any participation in the proceedings. Furthermore, as a crowning indignity, they were forced to sit in a balcony behind a curtain, screened from public gaze.

Speechless with anger, Mrs. Mott and Mrs. Stanton walked out of the hall. They discussed the calling of a women's equal rights rally once they were back in America. They corresponded and kept the idea alive through occasional meetings without taking any definite action. Mrs. Stanton had moved to Seneca Falls and was having babies regularly.

In 1848, a year that saw New York pass a law giving women certain property rights, the two friends met again. Mrs. Mott had come to the Finger Lakes country to attend a meeting of Hicksite Quakers and to visit her sister, Mrs. Martha Wright in Auburn.

Seneca Falls was only a short distance away and at Mrs. Stanton's home the two women returned to the topic they had first discussed in London, the calling of a convention to proclaim a new status for women.

Seated around a table in the Waterloo home of Quaker Richard Hunt, Mrs. Mott, Mrs. Stanton, Mrs. Wright, Jane Hunt and Mrs. Mary Ann McClintock drafted an announcement which appeared in the semi-weekly Seneca County Courier of July 14, 1848.

It told of a woman's rights convention to be held on July 19 and 20 in the Wesleyan Chapel in Seneca Falls and stated that the first day's session would be exclusively for women. The public was invited to the second day's meeting which would be addressed by Lucretia Mott and others.

Five days later crowds on foot and in carriages converged

on the Wesleyan Chapel. When the leaders of the convention arrived, they found the doors barred. A young nephew of Mrs. Stanton (he later became a professor at Yale) was hoisted through an open window and unlocked the door.

There were many men in the crowd and although the first session had been advertised "for women only," a hasty council around the altar decided not only to let the men stay but to invoke their help in the proceedings.

So tall, dignified James Mott, Lucretia's husband, in his gray Quaker clothes, was made presiding officer. Among the several speakers was Frederick Douglass, the Negro leader, then publishing his abolitionist paper in Rochester.

The instigators of the "revolution" had drawn up a manifesto modeled on the American Declaration of Independence. For the words, "the present King of Great Britain," the general term, "Man," was substituted. Then the Declaration went into a long recital of wrongs.

The tyrant Man, the Declaration charged, withheld from women the right of suffrage and compelled her to submit to laws in the formation of which she had no voice. He made her, if married, civilly dead in the eyes of the law. He took from her all rights in property, even to the wages she earned. He made her morally an irresponsible being—compelled to promise obedience to a husband who was to all intents and purposes her master.

There were other grievances against the tyrant Man. He taxed single women, if property owners, to support a government which did not otherwise recognize them. He barred to women the avenues to wealth and distinction which he enjoyed, leaving her only unprofitable employments. He denied her opportunities for education; gave her a subordinate position in the church; supported a double code of morals and "usurping the prerogative of Jehovah himself, claimed the

11

right to assign her a sphere of action when that belongs to her conscience and her God."

On top of this ringing manifesto the Seneca Falls convention adopted 11 resolutions, demanding among other things, the right to free education, equality with men in business and the professions; the right of free speech and to participate in public affairs and the right to vote. Only the last proviso was not adopted unanimously.

Sixty-eight women and 33 men signed the resolutions. Later some of them repudiated their signatures when a storm of ridicule broke on the heads of the leaders of the "Hen Convention."

Generally the press was unsparing in its derision. The *Rochester Democrat* commented that "the great effort seemed to bring out some new impracticable, absurd and ridiculous proposition and the greater the absurdity the better."

But James Gordon Bennett's *New York Herald* declared that "we are much mistaken if Lucretia Mott would not have made a better president than some of those who have lately tenanted the White House." In 1848 James K. Polk was serving his last year as President. He succeeded John Tyler in 1845.

The rebels against the status quo found the two days of the Seneca Falls pow-wow insufficient for the steam they had to let off. So they adjourned, to meet again in Rochester in two weeks.

The Rochester meeting had been well publicized and on Aug. 2, 1848 the Unitarian Church, then in North Fitzhugh Street, was filled to overflowing.

Against the advice of Mrs. Mott and Mrs. Stanton, a woman, Mrs. Abigail Bush, had been chosen to preside. It was feared that women's ignorance of parliamentary procedure and their inexperience in public meetings might

12

cause the conclave to break up in confusion, for there were hecklers and skeptics in the crowd.

But when some of the women secretaries could not make themselves heard, the strong, clear voice of Sarah Burtis, used to calling her school children to order, took charge and after that there was no hitch in the proceedings. It also is recorded that Mrs. Bush presided "with dignity and grace."

There were many speeches and more resolutions, one of them directed at the low wages paid women in Rochester.

The Seneca Falls and Rochester meetings were the Lexington and Concord of the women's "revolution." It was 72 years later, and all the leaders of the 1848 revolt were in their graves, when women finally achieved their supreme objective, the right of suffrage. But during those years, faced by hostility and ridicule, step by step, woman improved her status until the grievances against the tyrant Man, recited in the Seneca Falls Declaration of Independence, were no more.

The one time Wesleyan Chapel is an automobile salesroom now and on the side of the building is a plaque that tells that the first blow for emancipation of womanhood was struck there at the "Hen Convention" more than a century ago.

*   *   *

When late in 1848 young Susan Anthony left her teaching chores in Canajoharie for a brief visit to her Rochester home, she was surprised to hear that her parents and sister, Mary, had not only attended the second woman's rights convention but had joined the movement.

At that time Susan was deeply interested in temperance and abolition but equal rights left her cold. She was to learn that most of the leaders in the new cause also were temperance and anti-slavery reformers.

In 1852 Miss Anthony attended a state Sons of Temperance meeting in Albany as a delegate. When she rose to speak on a motion before the session, she was told that women were there to listen and to learn, not to speak. Stung by the rebuff, she arranged a state temperance meeting for women, to be held in Rochester.

At that convention the first state women's temperance society in the country was organized with Elizabeth Cady Stanton as its president. That daring woman made the proposal that drunkenness be made legal grounds for divorce.

Susan Anthony met Elizabeth Stanton for the first time at that convention. Each was drawn to the other and there began the long friendship and alliance that was to last as long as the two women lived.

Elizabeth was 37 years old, Susan five years her junior. Their temperaments were as different as were their backgrounds. They were as one in their devotion to a cause.

Elizabeth Cady was born in Johnstown in 1815, the daughter of a district judge. She was a member of a privileged class that never knew hardship, and she enjoyed unusual educational advantages for her time. As a girl she was tutored at home in Latin and Greek and later attended the pioneering Emma Willard School for young women at Troy. She mingled with intellectual people, developed social grace and was possessed of an easy flow of words.

Before her marriage, there seems to have been an unhappy love affair involving clandestine meetings with her brother-in-law, Edward Bayard of Seneca Falls. When she was 25 years years old, Elizabeth married Henry B. Stanton, a lawyer of liberal bent, who was an agent for the Anti-Slavery Society. They settled in a comfortable, well-shaded house on Washington Avenue, across the Seneca River from the village business district. It still stands. Elizabeth mothered seven children.

She was short, plump, curly haired, with charm and magnetism galore. She was a facile writer, an excellent speaker, skilled in debate and poised on any platform.

Susan Brownell Anthony was born at Adams, Mass., in the Berkshires, in 1820, of Quaker stock. Her father, the operator of a cotton mill, was not wealthy, but was comfortably off. Susan was a precocious and strong-willed child. She learned to read and write at the age of five and at a tender age was demanding to be taught long division. She was sent to a school for young ladies near Philadelphia and detested the regimentation of the place.

The panic of 1837 sent her father's fortunes into a tailspin and Susan earned her way by teaching school. The strong-limbed young woman put down a revolt of farm louts in a district school by scourging their leader with a stick she had cut in the woods.

In 1845 the Anthonys came to Rochester by canal boat and took over a 36-acre farm on the outskirts of the city, at about the present Brooks Avenue and Genesee Park Boulevard. Susan called Rochester home for the rest of her days. Actually it was only a base of operations, for the indefatigable warrior was eternally on the road, carrying the equal rights banner to distant battlefields.

In Canajoharie, where she had plenty of beaux, she was remembered as "a fine figure of a woman." She was five feet, six inches tall, well knit, with broad shoulders. She possessed great physical stamina. In the early years of their friendship, Mrs. Stanton referred to her as "that stately Quaker girl." Susan had brown hair, keen, gray eyes, a generous mouth, a strong chin and a broad brow. If in later years her expression was rather grim—she had been through a lot. The embattled spinster liked nice clothes and in her old age wore black silk with lace at the throat.

15

She was a human dynamo, with an analytical mind that got to the root of matters. She had a good memory and a gift for satire. She developed into an effective, but never showy, speaker. Earnestness and determination were the keynotes of her personality.

As the champions of reform, Mrs. Stanton supplied the words, Miss Anthony the action. Henry Stanton once said, "Stir up Susan and she stirs the world." His wife admitted that she "forged the thunderbolts and Susan fired them." When Elizabeth was inclined to let things drift, the younger woman prodded her into action. The single-minded spinster was even exasperated when her comrade's frequent child-bearing kept her away from the suffrage wars.

After their first meeting, the two women were much together, with Susan making frequent visits to the Stanton home in Seneca Falls. She was soon won over completely to the suffrage cause and to wearing the bloomers, the symbol of women's revolt. Susan and Mrs. Bloomer wore the costume during a temperance campaign they waged throughout the state in 1853. Two years later Mrs. Bloomer moved to Iowa. By that time the regalia was in the discard. Susan was one of the last to go back to long skirts.

During the 1850s equal rights, temperance and abolitionism shared the attentions of the "strong-minded females." In 1860 Mrs. Stanton and Miss Anthony sponsored a woman's rights rally in Albany and during it, Elizabeth appeared before a joint session of the Legislature to advocate legislation that made it possible for a woman to own, buy and sell property and make contracts. That measure passed. It was the first breach in the wall the tyrant Man had erected against the "weaker" sex.

Then the Civil War came and while the fate of the slaves was being settled on Southern battlefronts, Susan worked on the Rochester farm. She cooked, swept, planted, harvested and sold the crops, put up preserves and managed to attend what reform meetings were held.

After her father's death in 1862, Susan, her mother and sister moved into the brick house at 17 Madison Street in Rochester which today is a national shrine honoring the pioneer suffrage leader and to which Susan B. always returned from her campaigns.

During the war the Stantons moved to New York and Susan helped her friend get settled in her new home. The two masterminded a New York mass meeting at which Susan presented a resolution which demanded equal rights for Negro women, as well as men—and for all women, regardless of color. That last clause caused a furor, for some of the women did not want to go that far. The two leaders formed a Women's Loyal League, which obtained 100,000 names to a petition for the abolition of slavery. It was presented to the Senate by Charles Sumner, the Massachusetts abolitionist.

In the meantime the suffragists had organized the American Equal Rights Association which tied in a demand for votes for the Negro with a drive for equality for all women. The male abolitionist leaders, Wendell Phillips, Theodore Tilton and Frederick Douglass, would have none of it. It was the Negro's hour, they argued, and the women could wait. The suffragists felt they had been betrayed by their erstwhile allies.

Then came a split in their own ranks, with a conservative New England wing, led by Lucy Stone and Julia Ward Howe, breaking with the Stanton-Anthony forces, who formed a new group, the National Suffrage Association. That rift was not healed until 1888.

A factor that brought on the division was the alliance of the flamboyant, eccentric and wealthy George Francis Train

17

with the suffrage movement. He campaigned with Mrs. Stanton and Miss Anthony in the West and put on a gaudy show. He also financed a militant suffrage paper, the *Revolution,* which Miss Anthony managed, with Mrs. Stanton the chief editorial writer. Then Train took off for a long stay in Europe, leaving Susan holding the bag. She suspended the paper after a few months—with a deficit of $10,000. She paid off the debt unaided, with the proceeds of a strenuous lecture tour through the West.

In the early 1870s the two leaders became involved indirectly in the greatest scandal of the day. Theodore Tilton, idealistic editor, and his wife, Elizabeth, were friends of Mrs. Stanton and Miss Anthony in New York. It was from Elizabeth Tilton's lips that Susan heard the story of the young wife's illicit relations with her pastor, Henry Ward Beecher, the most famous pulpit orator in America.

Susan told Mrs. Stanton, pledging her to secrecy. But Elizabeth Stanton never could keep a secret. She had fallen under the spell of an adventuress named Virginia Woodhull, who, with her equally unscrupulous sister, Tennie Claflin, published a New York scandal sheet. Mrs. Stanton told the story of the Beecher-Tilton liasion to Virginia and soon it came out in *Woodhull's & Claflin's Weekly* and caused a national sensation.

Then the ambitious Mrs. Woodhull tried to take over the suffrage movement and even announced herself as a candidate for President on a People's ticket. Mrs. Stanton appeared helpless before the Woodhull assault but Susan B. was made of sterner stuff. Returning from a Western tour, she sized up the situation and when Virginia Woodhull took the floor and sought to control a suffrage meeting, the doughty Miss Anthony shut her off and ordered the lights in the hall turned off. She was vexed over Mrs. Stanton's conduct in the affair, but the two quickly made up.

In 1872 Susan B. Anthony plunged boldly into the national limelight. At the head of 13 women, including two of her sisters, she appeared in the polling place in a shoe shop at West Main and Prospect Streets in Rochester, demanded and obtained the right to register the 14 for the election. The word spread and some 50 women in various districts of the city registered.

But on election day only the 14 women who had registered in Miss Anthony's ward were allowed to vote. Their ballots were challenged and all were placed under arrest. Susan wanted to be sent to jail and refused to post the $1,000 bond demanded. But her counsel, Judge Henry R. Selden, raised the money rather than see his client in a cell.

The trial of the case of The People vs Susan B. Anthony, accused of the crime of voting in defiance of the law, was transferred from Monroe County to Canandaigua, seat of Ontario County. Miss Anthony packed in 21 speeches in that county before the trial began on July 17, 1873, before a crowded court room, Federal Judge Ward Hunt presiding.

Miss Anthony's lawyers, Judge Selden and John Van Voorhis, argued eloquently but in vain. Judge Hunt had his decision already written. He refused to let the jury pass on the evidence and directed a verdict of guilty. He sentenced the defendant to pay a fine of $100 and costs. Susan never paid either. She hoped to be sent to prison. But Judge Hunt, an experienced Republican politician, had no intention of making a martyr of the famous suffragist. The trial gave tremendous publicity to the equal rights cause.

During the 1880s and well into the 1890s, Miss Anthony bore the brunt of the campaigning. Tireless, she ranged the country. She saw her meetings broken up. She knew taunts and ridicule. She never faltered. She called on every new President. She presented her memorials to Congress and to the national political conventions, knowing they would be pigeonholed. Politicians knew they could not fool her logical mind and they feared her caustic tongue.

Horace Greeley was to feel its lash. During a conference, the editor asked Susan, sarcastically:

"Miss Anthony, you are aware the ballot and the bullet go together? If you vote, are you prepared to fight?"

Susan B. flashed back: "Certainly, Mr. Greeley, just as you fought in the late war—at the end of a goose quill."

Horace Greeley was cool to her the rest of his life.

The 1880s found the suffrage leaders busy. Mrs. Stanton, Miss Anthony and Matilda Gage collaborated in compiling the three-volume *History of Woman Suffrage,* a stupendous task. In October of 1881 Susan B. helped Clara Barton found in Rochester the second chapter of the American Red Cross. Miss Barton had organized the first chapter in Dansville in May of 1881.

During the 1890s Mrs. Stanton had grown too old and stout for much activity but her pen was far from idle. Always a rebel against organized religion, her hostility increased in her later years.

Although maintaining a rigorous schedule, Susan was spending more time in Rochester. In February, 1897, some 2,000 of her fellow townspeople gathered in Powers Hall to honor her on her 77th birthday. That wouldn't have happened 20 years earlier. Suffragists had become more respectable. There was less jeering. Several Western states had granted women the ballot. Susan B. knew the road ahead was long and rocky.

In 1899 she journeyed to London for an international women's meeting and met Queen Victoria. Susan shook hands with the Widow of Windsor American fashion and said briskly: "How do you do." She had forgotten that court etiquette called for her to kneel and kiss the monarch's hand. Or had she? She wasn't much of a hand for kneeling and kissing hands.

In the late 1890s Susan B. spearheaded the fight for the admission of women to the University of Rochester. In her youth she had spoken up for co-education in colleges at a teachers' meeting. The University of Rochester trustees had voted to accept women students on condition the city's women's organizations raise a $100,000 endowment fund before September of 1900.

When in June only $40,000 had been subscribed, the goal was reduced to $50,000. Miss Anthony led the desperate drive for that last $10,000. With all but $2,000 in hand and the deadline hours away, she pledged her own life insurance to make up the deficit.

That night exultant future co-eds carried great bouquets of flowers to the Anthony home. After the girls had left, Miss Anthony fell in a faint. She had suffered a slight stroke. The campaign had sapped her vitality. She was 80 years old. At the end of that memorable day, she wrote in her journal, in a shaky hand unlike her usual bold script: "They let the girls in."

In 1900 she resigned as president of the suffrage association. Younger women took the helm. But the old crusader kept a watchful eye on things, attended all the national conventions, an influential and venerated figure.

In June of 1902 she visited Mrs. Stanton for the last time. The old lady was nearly blind but with the help of a secretary she kept up her writing, especially her tirades against orthodox religion. Four months after Susan's visit, Elizabeth was dead at the age of 87.

Miss Anthony had always looked up to her friend's superior erudition, literary and speaking abilities, her tact and charm. But Susan was the stronger character of the two. She was a rock and sometimes Elizabeth was shifting sand.

Susan B. Anthony was not merely the sour-faced spinster, the iron-willed doctrinaire that the world knew. Underneath was a warmly human woman. She had a wide streak of tolerance in her makeup. Born in the strait-laced Quaker faith, she became a member of the liberal Unitarian Church.

During the Chicago World's Fair of 1893, in which women and Susan Anthony played a conspicuous part, the issue of Sunday opening arose. Susan took the liberal side. When a horrified clergyman asked her: "Would you allow a young man to go to a Wild West show on Sunday?" she answered: "Of course. In my opinion he would learn more from Buffalo Bill than from an intolerant sermon."

Colonel Buffalo Bill Cody had been her neighbor in Rochester. Hearing of her quip, the colonel sent her tickets for a box at one of his performances. When the old scout opened his show by riding in under a spotlight, he reined in his animal to its haunches in front of Miss Anthony's party and struck off his sombrero with a flourish. Susan rose and for a full minute the crowd cheered the showman and the suffragist, two remarkable personalities.

Miss Anthony in her old age attended the Women's World Congress in Berlin and had a long chat with the German Empress, who insisted that the famous American remain seated.

During her crowded lifetime Susan B. knew foreign royalty and every President from Grant to Theodore Roosevelt but she never lost the common touch. She would stop to chat with an old Negro as graciously as she would greet a lord mayor.

In 1906 she attended the national suffrage convention in Baltimore. She made a speech, her last one, and its peroration epitomized her whole career: "Failure is impossible." The 86-year-old gladiator took a cold at the convention and went home to Rochester to die.

Before she lapsed into a coma in the brick house in Madison Street, she called the roll of old comrades in the cause. All of them but one had gone before her to the other shore. Early on the morning of March 14, 1906 Susan Brownell Anthony passed away.

Leaders of the suffrage movement and local notables spoke at the funeral, held in Central Presbyterian Church amid a blizzard. Ten thousand people filed past her bier, at which stood University girls as a guard of honor.

Susan B. had been sleeping in Mount Hope for 14 years before the battle to which she had devoted her life was finally won. It was fitting that the law which gave women the right to vote was called the Susan B. Anthony Amendment.

Last of all her contemporaries to go was Elizabeth Smith Miller, the original "Bloomer Girl," who had come to live in Geneva with her banker husband in 1868. They had a beautiful estate, Lochland, at Geneva's southern edge. There Charles Dudley Miller died in 1896 but Elizabeth lived until 1911. To the last she retained her interest in women's rights and she was instrumental in founding William Smith College for Women at Geneva.

It seems sad that she had not lived to see the ultimate triumph of the cause of which the bloomers she first wore back in '51 were a symbol.

Chapter 3

First Lady Doctor

It was Tuesday, January 23, 1849, and the snow-clad Finger Lakes country sparkled in warm and welcome sunshine. In the village of Geneva crowds converged on the Presbyterian Church with its six Ionic columns. Soon all the pews and the galleries were filled. Women predominated in the audience.

The occasion was the commencement exercises of Geneva College, pioneer institution of higher learning in Western New York. After nearly 100 men had marched to the rostrum in groups of four to receive their diplomas from President Benjamin Hale, a slender young woman walked up the aisle alone.

She was no giddy young glamor girl but a dignified, self possessed, well formed young woman of 28, in a black silk dress with a silver brooch at her throat. Her fair, straight hair, severely combed, framed a strong face, with a determined chin and steady blue-gray eyes.

The crowded church had stirred when her name was called. For this was the moment most of them, especially the ladies, had been waiting for. It was the climax of the ceremonies. It also was a historic moment.

For the slim, serious girl, Elizabeth Blackwell, that day

received at Geneva the first medical diploma ever granted a woman.

Thus history again was made in the Finger Lakes country, cradle of women's suffrage, where the year before at Seneca Falls, a few miles away, the first equal rights convention in America had met and where women were for the first time to wear the daring bloomer costume, symbolic of their cause.

Elizabeth Blackwell did not belong to the Bloomer Brigade. She wore conventional clothes although she never cared much what she wore. But she held unorthodox beliefs. One of them was that women had the right to practice medicine. And her triumph over tradition and prejudice in winning recognition for her sex in a field hitherto barred to women marked a significant milestone along the long road to emancipation.

That Geneva College diploma launched Miss Blackwell on a remarkable trail-blazing career. One of her biographers summed up her "firsts" in this way:

"She was the first woman in history to graduate from a medical college, first to enter an American hospital as an interne, first to be enrolled on the medical register of Great Britain, founded the first school of nursing in America."

She was born in Bristol, England, in 1821, one of a family of nine. Several of her brothers and sisters also were destined for fame. Her father, Samuel Blackwell, the prosperous owner of a sugar refinery, belonged to the Independent Church, a denomination akin to the Quakers. He was interested in various reform movements and dared to voice his belief that women were entitled to the same educational opportunities as men.

Elizabeth and her sisters were taught by governesses at home such unusual subjects for their sex and time as history, mathematics, Latin and Greek grammar. The little girl,

25

who even in babyhood had a determined way about her, showed no interest in embroidery and other fashionable and purely feminine arts.

The family emigrated to New York in 1832. Samuel Blackwell opened a sugar refinery and the family joined the anti-slavery agitation. The panic of 1837 ruined the Blackwell business and the family moved to Cincinnati, where the father died in 1839, leaving little estate and nine children.

Elizabeth and two sisters opened a day school for girls in their home. "Elib," as she was known to her family, was restless, ambitious and scornful of the role custom decreed for her sex. She did not like teaching but she did her share. In Cincinnati the Blackwells met distinguished people, including Harriet Beecher Stowe, the author of *Uncle Tom's Cabin,* and others of the Beecher clan.

In her *Autobiographical Sketches* written in England when she was 74 years old, Miss Blackwell recalled of the Cincinnati period of her life that:

"The wider education of women was a subject then coming to the fore and we three sisters threw ourselves into the public conferences."

Then Elizabeth went to Mississippi to teach a little backwoods school, a grim experience.

A turning point in her life came when on her return to Cincinnati a woman friend, victim of an incurable, malignant disease, whom she nursed, said:

"You are fond of study. You have health and leisure. Why not study medicine? If I could have been treated by a lady doctor, my worst sufferings would have been spared me."

At first she brushed away the idea as fantastic but it kept bobbing up in her mind. She had a natural inclination toward medicine and service to humanity. And there was another factor which determined her course. This frank passage in her autobiography reveals Elizabeth Blackwell as a very human woman back of her self imposed facade of imperturbability:

"I became impatient of the disturbing influence exercised by the other sex. I had always been extremely susceptible to this influence. I never remember the time from first adoration at seven years of a little boy with rosy cheeks and flaxen curls that I had not suffered more or less from the common malady—falling in love. But when I became sufficiently intimate with an individual to realize what a life association might mean, I shrank from the prospect, disappointed or repelled. . . . I felt more determined than ever to become a physician and thus place a strong barrier between me and all ordinary marriage."

She lived to the age of 89 and never married.

So in 1845 she began the long struggle to batter down one of the most formidable barriers then facing a woman, to become a doctor. At the onset, she had little idea of the obstacles in her path.

First she must gain entrance to a medical college, something no woman had ever done. Confidently she began writing letters to influential friends, many of them physicians. Every one of them tried to dissuade her from her plan, which they called impossible.

In the meantime she had to make her living. She taught a year in a girls' school in Asheville, N.C. There the minister who conducted the school tutored her in physics and chemistry and the theory of anatomy. Then she taught in a fashionable boarding school in Charleston, S.C. where she studied medicine in the evenings under a professor of the local medical school. But her efforts to enroll in that and other schools met with rebuffs.

In the Summer of 1847 she went with her hard-won sav-

27

ings to Philadelphia, the seat of medical learning in the United States. She was sure she could get into one of the four medical schools there. She interviewed professor after professor and received little encouragement and generally outright rejection.

She began anatomical studies in a private school and gained valuable experience. She overcame her first squeamishness in the dissecting room, went about her work serenely and methodically and won the grudging respect of her male associates.

Still the rejections came in—from Harvard, Bowdoin and even the smallest medical schools in the East. Elizabeth never gave up. She had faith in ultimate success. She was not impressed by the advice of her Quaker physician friend, Dr. Warrington:

"Thee cannot gain admission to these schools. Thee must go to Paris and don masculine attire to gain the necessary knowledge."

Miss Blackwell's answer was: "I am embarked on a moral crusade, a course of justice and common sense and it must be pursued in the light of day and with public sanction."

Among the schools to which she had applied was a small medical college at Geneva, a village of 4,000 on the shores of Seneca Lake in Upstate New York. Geneva College, chartered in 1825 and soon to be renamed Hobart in honor of its founder, the Episcopal Bishop, John Henry Hobart, had opened a pioneering medical department in 1836.

In late October Elizabeth Blackwell was electrified to open a letter postmarked Geneva, N.Y. and to read, under the signature of Charles A. Lee, dean of the faculty, these words:

"I am instructed by the faculty of the medical department

of Geneva College to acknowledge yours of the 3d inst. A quorum of the faculty assembled last evening . . . and it was thought important to submit your proposal to the class of students, who have had a meeting this day, and acted entirely on their own behalf, without interference on the part of the faculty. I send you the result of their deliberations, and need only to add that there are no fears, but that you can, by judicious management, not only 'disarm criticism,' but elevate yourself without detracting in the least from the dignity of your profession. . . ."

Enclosed was a copy of the resolution unanimously adopted Oct. 20, 1847 by the medical class:

"Resolved—That one of the radical principles of a republican government is the universal education of both sexes; that to every branch of scientific education the door should be open equally to all; that the application of Elizabeth Blackwell to become a member of our class meets our entire approbation; and in extending our unanimous invitation, we pledge ourselves that no conduct of ours shall cause her to regret her attendance at this institution."

A radiant Elizabeth, "with an immense sigh of relief and feelings of profound gratitude instantly accepted the invitation and prepared for the journey to Western New York State."

She did not then know that when the students voted on her application, some of them thought the whole thing was a joke inspired by a rival school and shouted "aye" in a prankish spirit. However, the tone of the resolution indicates a liberal sentiment and serious thought on the part of the majority.

The step the Geneva students had taken was a courageous, as well as a revolutionary one. For in 1847 the very idea of a woman studying medicine, rolling pills, taking pulses, delivering babies was fantastic.

* * *

Elizabeth traveled all night from Philadelphia to reach Geneva on the evening of November 6. In later years she recalled that "the next morning I sallied forth for an interview with the dean of the college, enjoying the view of the beautiful lake on which Geneva is situated, notwithstanding the cold, drizzly, windy day." She was enrolled as student 130 on the list of the medical department.

That department was housed in a brick building, whose cupola was dwarfed by the nearby tower of Trinity Church, cradle of the Episcopal faith in Western New York. The medical building, on the Seneca Lake side of South Main Street, was erected in 1841-42.

There was then, as there is today, an air of distinction and a cultural tone about Geneva, one of the oldest settlements in the region and the trading center for a rich farming section. Even in pioneer days Geneva was described as "an elegant and salubrious village."

Elizabeth Blackwell found this comely town not too cordial toward newcomers, especially those who flouted ancient taboos. Diehards of the old regime, people who resented all change, condemned "those professors" for their advanced views, and specifically for letting a woman enroll in the medical school.

Her first days in Geneva were lonely ones. She found a room in a boarding house near the college, but, as she wrote her sister, "there was not a soul to speak to." The shy girl wandered about "the great building," (the medical school), occasionally got lost, for three days before she was admitted to a classroom.

30

At first the students and the villagers regarded her as a sort of a freak. The path of a lone rebel against convention is never easy. It was the plump, jolly little professor of anatomy, Dr. James Webster, who first made her feel at home. He encouraged her in her desire to study surgery, despite the shocked objection of Dean Lee.

She was so business-like and unobtrusive that the male students soon accepted her. They began to call her "Blackwell," as if she were a fellow male.

Early she manifested her independent spirit. When a professor sought to bar her from a lecture because it involved witnessing an operation "of a delicate nature," she penned him a letter in which she pointed out she was a registered student, had paid her full tuition fee, and was entitled to take part in all class work. She wound up her manifesto with the declaration that "all parts of the human body are holy within the sight of God. Nor are the pangs of disease biased."

The professor read her letter to her fellow students and put the decision up to them. Unanimously they voted that she attend the lecture. When she entered the ampitheater for the demonstration, they rose and cheered her.

But in the village she still was the object of curiosity and some malicious gossip. Some Geneva ladies seemed to regard her as a sort of "fancy woman," instead of a serious-minded student of medicine. All stared at her. Some snubbed her. Elizabeth wrote home that "when the great doors of the college closed behind me, they shut off all unfriendly criticism."

Visitors came to Geneva to see this remarkable young woman. A Springfield newspaper sent a reporter who wrote that "Miss Blackwell comes into the class with great composure, takes off her bonnet and puts it under the seat, exposing a fine phrenology. Great decorum is observed while she is present."

She spent the Summer in the women's hospital ward of the Blockley Almshouse in Philadelphia, which was full of Irish emigrants stricken with the typhus known as "famine fever." Elizabeth wrote her thesis about that disease, "studying in the midst of the poor dying sufferers." The male resident junior physicians tried at first to embarrass her, but she went her cool, detached, efficient way, as she had at Geneva, and soon she was one of them.

She returned to Geneva in the Autumn and presented her thesis which was acclaimed by Doctor Webster and the students. When graduation time rolled around in January, 1849, some question arose as to whether a lone woman should receive her diploma with the men of the class. Doctor Webster came to Miss Blackwell's defense, stoutly arguing that she had paid her tuition and passed her courses with honors. Her name went on the roll of graduates.

The commencement ceremonies traditionally were held in Trinity Church but the Presbyterian Church was chosen in 1849, perhaps out of deference to Elizabeth's affiliation with that denomination.

Her tall dignified brother, George, came to Geneva for the event. People flocked into town from the hinterlands and all Geneva turned out to see "the lady doctor" receive her sheepskin. Elizabeth declined to walk in the academic procession from campus to church on the ground "it would not be ladylike." She and her brother went ahead of the others and took seats in the rear of the church, so that Elizabeth might join the procession as it marched in.

The lone woman in the class was the last called to the platform and she went up alone. After President Hale

32

handed her the hard-won diploma, she bowed, started to walk away, then turned back and said in a clear voice:

"Sir, I thank you; by the help of the Most High it shall be the effort of my life to shed honor on your diploma." Hale bowed, the audience applauded.

Then Dean Lee in his address alluded to Elizabeth's intelligence and dignified and lady-like deportment which, he said, "has proved that the strongest intellect and nerve and the most untiring perseverance are compatible with the softest attributes of delicacy and grace." The students applauded that pronouncement.

It had been a proud day for Elizabeth Blackwell. Before she boarded a train that night, her room was crowded with visitors. Some of them were the same people who had snubbed her. She wrote years later: "My past experience had given me a useful and permanent lesson at the outset of life on the very shallow nature of popularity."

She never returned to Geneva in the flesh but her autobiography indicates that the school along Seneca's water and her 27 weeks with her Alma Mater were often in her thoughts. She kept up a correspondence with Doctor Webster and other Geneva friends, and was delighted to meet Dean Lee in Paris the next year.

*   *   *

The rest of Elizabeth Blackwell's long life was almost a continual battle against prejudice as the indomitable woman blazed new trails in medicine.

Three weeks after her graduation, she was off for Paris to study surgery. In France she ran into the same old walls. She was a woman. Therefore she was denied admission to the hospitals as a post graduate student. Finally she had to enter the woman's hospital, La Maternite, as a common nursing apprentice.

There while she was treating a baby, medicine from a syringe spilled into her eye. She lost the sight of that eye, dashing her hopes of becoming a surgeon. She became ill and visited the water cures. But she never gave up.

In 1850, through the help of an English cousin, she began work and study in St. Bartholomew's Hospital in London. But she was barred from the department of female diseases.

Returning to New York the next year, she rented an office but the landlady would not allow a woman doctor's sign on the premises. She moved to Washington Square but encountered the same edict. She sat in her office waiting for the patients that never came. Finally she went to Horace Greeley, famous editor of the *New York Tribune,* with a notice she had written announcing her opening of an office. That violated the code of medical ethics but the liberal-minded Greeley ran it.

Then the patients came. Elizabeth lectured. She campaigned for a medical college for women only, the harder after Geneva College, her own alma mater, had refused to admit sister Emily. Later, Western Reserve took Emily in and she got her medical degree from that Ohio college. Emily was to be associated for years with her older sister Elizabeth.

(The Blackwells were a remarkable family. Of the five sisters, none of whom married, two became physicians, one an artist and author, another a musician, and the fifth was denied a public career because of ill health. Two brothers married women who won fame as crusaders. Henry, who became rich and was active in the anti-slavery and suffrage movements, married pretty Lucy Stone, a leading feminist, whose insistence on retaining her maiden name after marriage created a vogue.

(Brother Samuel married Antoinette Brown, a native of Henrietta, whose career in another field paralleled Elizabeth Blackwell's in medicine. In the late 1840s the quiet, determined Miss Brown applied for entrance in the theological course at Oberlin College. Women preachers were as rare as women doctors in those days. Reluctantly the officials finally yielded and Antoinette Brown was graduated with the class of 1850. But her name was omitted from the published list of graduates. For three years she sought a pulpit. In 1853 she got into the limelight when she, an accredited delegate to the World Temperance Convention in New York, was not allowed to speak—only because she was a woman. A few days later she was ordained and took the pastorate of the little Congregational Church in South Butler, Wayne County. Shortly she switched to the Unitarians and became a leader in the feminist cause.)

Emily, now a full-fledged surgeon, joined Elizabeth in New York where they opened a free clinic for indigent women and children in a little room, which in 1857 was expanded into the New York Infirmary and College for Women, a hospital and school conducted by and for women. Dressed in worn clothes, her mind only on her cause, Elizabeth spoke at rallies and raised funds for the Infirmary.

The sisters opened the first nursing school in America. They had to battle ignorance, misery and filth in their New York trail-blazing. Most of their patients were foreign-born. Once they were stoned and insulted by a mob, after an emigrant woman had died in their hospital of inflammation of the appendix, which was inevitably fatal in that age.

Back to her native England went Elizabeth in the Summer of 1858. Her reception was more cordial this time and she became the first woman to be enrolled on the Medical Register of Great Britain. Still she was barred from practicing in pediatrics or gynecology.

The year 1864 found Miss Blackwell again in New York, where one of her dreams came true with the organization of a women's medical college with a four-year course. For the first time disease prevention was taught and Elizabeth became a professor of hygiene on the faculty.

Soon the restless doctor was on the move again. She left sister Emily in charge of affairs in New York and again crossed the sea to England, this time to stay. In her homeland she became acquainted with such notables as Florence Nightingale, Charles Kingsley, George Eliot, Herbert Spencer. She preached the gospel of preventive medicine, advocating good food, freedom from worry, sunshine, exercise as cardinal rules. She introduced anesthesia and developed vaccines.

The public did not snap up all her theories. She determinedly put her health lectures in book form, conceding that "it may be I am writing for 1970, not 1870."

She organized a national English health society with the slogan, "Prevention is better than cure." She wrote a book of advice for parents which stirred controversy. Always serious, intense, dignified, without pomp or frills, she went her dedicated way.

The tired eyes shone when she learned that on the 50th anniversary of her graduation from Geneva College, the first dormitory of the new William Smith College for Women on the old remembered campus had been named Blackwell House in her honor. That was in 1899.

Elizabeth Blackwell died at Hastings, England, in 1910, at the age of 89. She sleeps in the churchyard of the hamlet of Kilmum, Argyllshire, Scotland.

On January 24, 1949, just 100 years after the happy day

she received her degree at Geneva, the co-ordinated Colleges of the Seneca, Hobart and William Smith, marked the anniversary with a convocation at which 12 eminent women physicians from the United States, Canada, France and England received citations.

In the early 1940s Hollywood prepared a movie based on the life of the "First Lady Doctor." But the second World War came on and the script was shoved into some pigeonhole.

Let us hope that one day it will be brought out and on the screen a slim, serious girl in a black bonnet will trudge again down Geneva's South Main Street, her arms full of text books; that this generation may know a remarkable woman's life-long fight against prejudice, disease and ignorance.

One word symbolizes the life of Elizabeth Blackwell and that word is DETERMINATION.

Chapter 4

Conductors on the Underground

He won great fame and lives in the history books as Frederick Douglass. But that was not his real name, merely a fancy monicker a white abolitionist picked out from the works of Sir Walter Scott.

To his white masters and his fellow slaves in Talbot County, on Maryland's Eastern Shore, where he was born, he was Fred Bailey. As a child he lived with his grandparents and their name was Bailey. Of course he never knew the name of his white father. And he had only vague memories of hasty visits in the night from the tall, well-formed Negress who was his mother and who was sold and went away when he was very young.

Even the exact date of his birth is uncertain, but it was around February in 1817. He grew into a big, handsome boy with bright eyes and a massive head. There was no mistaking the white blood that flowed in his veins.

When he was a young boy, he lived in the "Big House" on the plantation and escaped the overseer's lash, although he saw others cruelly treated.

At the age of nine he went to live in Baltimore with a new master, Hugh Auld. Auld was basically a kindly man, and his wife took a liking to the alert boy and taught him to read and write. The Aulds' son became a friend and playmate. His six years in Baltimore were happy ones for Fred. He made enough money blacking boots on the side to buy his first book. Significantly it was the *Columbian Orator,* a compilation of notable speeches. Years later when Frederick Douglass was renowned as one of America's greatest orators, that book had an honor spot in the library of his home in Rochester.

The idyllic life in Baltimore ended when Fred was sent back to the country, to the plantation of Thomas Auld, Hugh's brother. There he saw slaves whipped and when he protested, he became known as an "uppity nigger." His master was furious when Fred was caught teaching other slaves to read and a white posse broke up a Sunday-school class he had organized. Finally the boy was turned over to a brute named Covey, who made his living "breaking in" unruly slaves.

At Covey's, he was beaten, half starved and subjected to insult. His proud spirit at length rebelled and Covey felt the sinewy hands of the slave youth at his throat. He called for help but none of the other hands responded, and Covey had to give in. This boy had been too much for the professional bully who had "broken in" so many other slaves.

After that Auld farmed Fred out to a planter named Freeland who, although far from prosperous, treated his people well. But Fred Bailey had determined to be free and with five others hatched a plan to escape by canoe down Chesapeake Bay. Douglass had written out passes for all six and the hour was set. Someone betrayed them and the six were rounded up and taken to jail.

Under the sting of the lash, the six denied they had planned to run away. At Fred's command, all had swallowed the passes he had written out. Finally the slave catchers had to release the youths for lack of evidence.

Fred Bailey's fortunes brightened when Thomas Auld sent him back to Baltimore to live with Hugh. He went to work in a ship yard as a calker, but the white hands abused him, once beating him unmercifully. Hugh Auld demanded that the attackers be prosecuted but the magistrate refused to swear out any warrant on the word of a Negro. That incident only increased Fred's resolve to be his own man.

He got a job in another shipyard and was allowed to keep a small part of the wages he earned. He saved every cent he could. He became active in a free Negro society in Baltimore and there he made his first public address. It was an awkward but earnest protest against proposed colonization of free Negroes in Africa. At these meetings he met slender, dark-eyed Anna Murray, born free. They fell in love and Fred promised to send for her after he had made his way to freedom.

Fred's escape plan was audacious. On Sept. 3, 1838, wearing the uniform of a United States sailor, he leaped aboard a train just as it was pulling out of Baltimore. He had with him a precious document, a federal sailor's "protection," embossed with the gold eagle of the Union. He had borrowed it from a free Negro who had served in the Navy. Luckily the conductor only glanced at the paper, saw the gold eagle and went on.

Within 24 hours Fred Bailey was in New York City. He had escaped from bondage but still was in danger of being returned to his master. In New York he got to know the leaders, white and black, of the Underground Railroad system that was spiriting many slaves across the line. He sent for Anna Murray and they were married by a Presbyterian minister.

Because many Southerners came to New York, his friends felt it was not a safe haven. So they sent him to New Bedford,

Mass., where he was to work in the ship yards. There he was taken under the wing of Nathan Johnson, an intelligent free Negro. It was Johnson who transformed Frederick Bailey into Frederick Douglass. He borrowed the new surname from Sir Walter Scott's "Lady of the Lake."

Even in New England, that hotbed of abolitionism, he found that white men would not work beside him on a equal footing. So he had to turn to odd jobs and common labor. He read *the Liberator,* the fiery abolition journal of William Lloyd Garrison and attended lectures at the Lyceum. He began speaking at meetings of the Negro community and gradually developed a platform poise.

For three years he studied and listened and learned much about the anti-slavery movement. He attracted the attention of white champions of the cause and in 1841 came a turning point in his career. It was at an anti-slavery rally in Nantucket and on the platform were Garrison and other notables. A friend, William C. Coffin, an agent for the Underground, came to Douglass and asked him to say a few words to the gathering. The abashed Negro demurred.

"Just tell them your story, Frederick, as you have told it so many times to me," Coffin urged.

So with simple, moving eloquence the young mulatto with the musical voice, the leonine head and the burning eyes told the story of what he had seen and suffered under slavery. His audience and Garrison were much impressed. After that Douglass became a much sought after speaker for the cause. He became an agent of the Massachusetts Anti-Slavery Society and made a speaking tour of the Northern states. And one day, in a Massachusetts town, he spoke for the first time alone—and did well.

He traveled through New York State, along the Erie Canal, in the Southern Tier, along Lake Ontario, through the Finger Lakes country. He met such friends of the cause as wealthy Gerrit Smith of Peterboro, the Rev. Samuel May in Syracuse and the Anthonys, Posts and the Porters in Rochester.

In the Middle West his path was strewn with rotten eggs, stones and insults. His advance was heralded by placards that screamed: "NIGGER FRED IS COMING," and hostile crowds were on hand to greet him. In Pendleton, Ind., he was beaten and left for dead. He suffered a serious arm injury in that affair. He was rebuffed at hotels, in restaurants and on trains because of his color. He was hissed and jeered at in meeting halls. He went his way, undaunted.

At first he confined his talks to the simple story of his life in bondage. Actually his lot had been easier than that of many another slave, but none other could speak so eloquently. During his tours and association with intellectuals, he became familiar with the political and economic aspects of the slavery issue, and he broadened his speeches to include those matters.

In 1845 a book came out in Boston, titled *Narrative of the Life of Frederick Douglass*. It aroused such feeling in the South that his friends feared Douglass would be taken back into slavery. So in August he sailed for England on the Cunard luxury liner, *the Cambria,* in the steerage.

He was warmly greeted in the British Isles, met some of the leading statesmen and became a fast friend of Daniel O'Connell, the Irish patriot. He addressed many meetings and won converts for his cause. He engendered a sympathy among the working classes that paid off when the Civil War came and Britain wavered between the combatants.

After 23 months abroad, he came home, a free man. Two Englishwomen had purchased his freedom from Thomas Auld.

An international figure now and with $2,500 raised for the cause in England, Douglass determined to set up his own abolitionist paper, but not in New England, the home of Garrison's *Liberator*. His old idol, Garrison, did not like the idea. He felt that another anti-slavery paper was not needed.

Despite the rift with Garrison, Douglass went ahead with his plans and in December 1847, the first issue of a four-page weekly, *the North Star*, came out in Rochester. Douglass had picked the Western New York city because of its liberal attitude and its location midway between New England and the West.

There is a tradition that the paper was founded in the basement of the African Methodist Episcopal Zion Church in Favor Street. For years the *North Star*, which later was renamed the *Frederick Douglass Paper*, was published from an office on the site of the present Wilder Building at Rochester's Four Corners.

Two Englishwomen of independent means, the sisters Julia and Eliza Griffis, came to Rochester to help Douglass with his paper and to live in the Douglass home at what was then 4 Alexander Street near East Avenue. The spectacle of the two white women walking arm in arm down Main Street with the Negro editor aroused some gossip in Rochester. Julia in particular gave valuable assistance. She helped Douglass with his writing and put the paper on a sound financial basis.

Gerrit Smith and other abolitionists helped Douglass, and the paper grew. James Gordon Bennett's *New York Herald*, however, recommended that the "white citizens of Rochester throw Frederick Douglass and his printing press into Lake Ontario."

Douglass was more than busy. He lectured in Rochester's Corinthian Hall and made speaking trips into Western New

York. Besides he was the local station master of the Underground and Rochester, on Lake Ontario facing Canada, was a key point in the system that carried so many Negro fugitives to liberty. More than 200 slaves passed through the city on the Underground each year.

The fugitives were spirited to Rochester by various routes, then put on lake boats at Charlotte, Pultneyville, Sodus Point, Parma and other ports. Sometimes they were hidden in piles of wood. Warsaw, Canandaigua, Fishers, Palmyra, Naples and many other Western New York places were stops on the freedom road.

In Rochester there were many havens, including Douglass' home on Alexander Street near East Avenue and his printing office. Runaways slept in the pews of the M. E. Zion Church, in the sail loft of Edward Williams near the Four Corners, in Samuel Porter's barn on South Fitzhugh Street, and the nearby pillared mansion where the Fox Sisters, high priestesses of Spiritualism once lived, although they had nothing to do with the Underground.

There was the farm home of the Anthonys far out on the West Side where a strong-minded teacher daughter named Susan came to live in 1849; the home of Grove S. Gilbert, the artist, on Greig Street; the Isaac Moore house at 1496 Culver Road where a secret chamber led to a tunnel; the home of William C. Bloss, the tavernkeeper who became a temperance reformer, at 28 East Avenue, and the residence of Dr. L. C. Dolley, next door.

The refugees hid in the cellar of a Parma store, in the Mihan house at Williamsville, in the cellar of the stately brick Hargous house in Pittsford and many another sanctuary known only to the inner circle. And there was the home of Gideon Pitts in Honeoye—which figures later in the Douglass story.

No fugitives were ever recovered by the slave catchers in Rochester, but there were some close calls.

Three Negroes came to the city and remained for months, unmolested. They even attended the anti-slavery meetings in Corinthian Hall. One night the word was passed that their master was in town, looking for a United States marshal and a warrant. For three days they were hidden in various places and at night, disguised as Quakeresses, in bonnets and veils, they were taken to Charlotte in a closed carriage and put aboard a waiting boat, while the marshal was hunting for them.

Again, three men who had been involved in the murder of a slave catcher in Pennsylvania, came to the Douglass home. Frederick acted swiftly, because there was a big reward out for the trio. He dressed them in women's garb, put them in a wagon and rushed them to the lake where they went aboard a Canadian boat, which had been engaged by the indefatigable Julia Griffis.

There were many abolitionists in Rochester and they raised considerable money to keep the Underground going. But they were in a minority and many of the conservative element looked down on them as crackpot fanatics.

Many stories of the Douglass years in the Genesee Country persist. His wife, Anna, was a shy, uneducated woman and the public activities of her distinguished husband were beyond her simple ken. She was content in her role of good wife and mother and model housekeeper. It was said that the presence of the Griffis sisters in her home and their close association with her husband irked her, and Garrison, after his break with Douglass, made ugly insinuations in his paper.

The Douglasses were popular with their neighbors, especially with the children who came to hear Fred play his violin and sing the songs of the Southland in his rich baritone.

Despite the impassioned fervor of his public speeches, Douglass was urbane and moderate in his manners and won the liking of most of the leading white citizens of Rochester.

The family ran into Jim Crowism in the Rochester public school system. Negro children could attend only the Colored School in North Washington Street. Hence the nearby Public School 15 was barred to the Douglass children. Rather than send them across town to the Colored School, Douglass, who was opposed to all forms of segregation, hired a teacher to instruct his children in his home.

At one time he placed his daughter Rosetta in a fashionable girls' private school. There she was segregated and made unhappy, and he had to withdraw her. He began a campaign for equal rights in the schools. Samuel Porter, the abolitionist, supported him and in 1857 the public schools of Rochester were opened to all children, regardless of color.

In his speeches he did not spare the clergy who gave the sanction of the church to the slave-holding system and thereby aroused some antagonism.

Before he settled in Rochester, Douglass had met in Springfield, Mass., a bearded woolen merchant, a fiery abolitionist, named John Brown. Brown told Douglass his scheme for freeing many slaves by maintaining small bands in the mountains near the border and raiding nearby plantations. It was not a large scale operation he outlined. Douglass approved the idea and he and Brown kept in communication with each other, although their paths separated.

In 1858, Brown, under the name of Nelson Hawkins, visited Douglass in the Negro leader's new home on South Avenue, just north of the Lily Pond in Highland Park. It was a secluded place, back from the street and sheltered by many trees. As the two men walked the hills, Brown unfolded a new plan for freeing slaves.

Its audacity and possible consequences appalled Douglass. Brown aimed to seize the United States arsenal at Harper's Ferry, Va., with an armed band, meanwhile calling on thousands of slaves to rise in revolt. The ever practical Douglass tried to dissuade the old fanatic from his scheme.

Douglass felt that the plan had little chance of success and he warned Brown that seizure of government property was an act of treason. The mad old man was adamant.

Three weeks before the date set for the Harper's Ferry raid, Brown summoned Douglass to a conference in Chambersburg, Pa. Douglass took along a giant Negro, an escaped slave named Shields Green, called by the blacks "Emperor" Green, because of a legend that his father had been a king in Africa. Green had found sanctuary with Douglass in Rochester.

The men met in a quarry in the Pennsylvania hills. Brown implored Douglass to join in the raid. Douglass would have nothing to do with the scheme and again warned of the possible consequences. When it came time to leave, Shields Green said quietly: "I stay with the old man."

He stayed and was caught with the rest of Brown's men when the federal troops under Capt. Robert E. Lee ended the insurrection at Harper's Ferry.

The news of the fiasco reached Douglass in Philadelphia where he was speaking. He was in grave danger, for in his home in Rochester there were incriminating letters from Brown. He telegraphed his son Lewis to get the papers from his high desk and hide them.

Douglass was linked to the conspiracy and his friends urged him to flee the country. When John Brown was executed, Douglass was safe in Canada. He fled just in time. United States marshals were in Rochester with a Virginia warrant within six hours of his flight. From Canada he sailed for England, where he waited for the storm to blow over. Five months later he was called home by the death of a daughter, Anna. There was no attempt to arrest him.

Douglass was an early member of the new Republican party and campaigned for John C. Fremont in 1856. He long had abandoned the Garrison idea of "moral suasion" for open political action in the fight against slavery.

The campaign of 1860 found him on the stump for Abraham Lincoln, although he had supported his friend, William H. Seward of Auburn, for the Republican nomination. After the war came, he worked to bring Negroes into the Union army, as soldiers, not as laborers. He called for emancipation of the slaves. Lincoln was not ready for either move, but in the White House he listened sympathetically to Douglass and the two men became friends, although they often differed on methods.

After the Union ranks were opened to Negroes, Douglass issued his famous call, "Men of Color, To Arms." He helped recruit the first two colored regiments and saw his sons, Lewis and Charles, march away. He won Lincoln over to commissioning Negro officers and was himself promised a commission by War Secretary Stanton. It never arrived. Before the war ended, nearly 187,000 had worn the Union blue and 92,000 others had served as civilians.

Douglass was the chief speaker at the civic mass meeting in Rochester that mourned the assassination of President Lincoln and his eloquence on that occasion lingered in many a memory. Mrs. Lincoln gave him a cane the President had carried and Douglass cherished it the rest of his life.

The Negro leader did not get along well with Andrew Johnson and did not agree with the new President's reconstruction program. He became allied with the Radical bloc in Congress, led by the vindictive Thaddeus Stevens, who wanted the South treated as a conquered province. Douglass worked only for complete freedom for his people. He was not interested in the lot of former slaveholders.

Douglass for years had been active in the equal rights movement, he had spoken at the historic first women's rights rally in Seneca Falls and had worked with Susan B. Anthony, Elizabeth Cady Stanton, Lucy Stone and the other women reformers, who also stood for temperance and against slavery.

Douglass parted company with his old associates, the suffragists, over the 14th Amendment which granted the Negroes equal citizenship. The women wanted the word "male" stricken from the qualification for voting. Douglass and his anti-slavery allies, including the silver-tongued Wendell Phillips, held that "it was the Negro's hour" and that other reforms could wait. Enfranchisement of women had to wait 50 years. In 1870 the women's rights leaders felt that Douglass was ungrateful for the help they had given him. But he never swerved from his goal, equal rights for his people. In later years he and his famous fellow Rochesterian, Susan B. Anthony, patched up their differences.

After the war Douglass was in Washington much of the time and he moved to the capital after fire destroyed his Rochester home near the present Highland Park in 1872. His family escaped but the Negro statesman's valuable papers and books were lost in the blaze. Douglass hastened home on learning of the fire. He arrived in Rochester by train around midnight and decided he would spend the rest of the night in a downtown hotel.

At the Congress Hall, the clerk, not recognizing the Negro at the desk, gave the stock answer: "No rooms left." At the other principal hotel, the Waverly, Douglass got the same treatment, until the proprietor came into the lobby, saw who was being turned away and upbraided his clerk. But Douglass, not caring to be accepted because of his prominence after he had been scorned because of his color, trudged through the rain to join his family, sheltered in a neighbor's home.

Because Douglass was the acknowledged spokesman for thousands of newly enfranchised voters, Republican Presidents showered offices on him. In 1877 President Hayes named him United States marshal for the District of Columbia, the highest federal position ever given a Negro.

Douglass accepted with alacrity, although it had been Hayes who withdrew from the freedmen of the South the protection of the federal troops during the reconstruction period. Hayes' action was in keeping with the deal that gave him the disputed Presidential election of 1876, in exchange for the end of carpetbagger rule in the South. William Lloyd Garrison and Wendell Phillips protested the move, but not Douglass. He settled down in a 21-room house in the suburbs of Washington.

In 1882 he was made recorder of deeds in the District. That was the year his wife, Anna, died. In 1884 Douglass was appointed minister to the black republic of Haiti. That was the year the 67-year-old leader of the Negroes married a white wife. His marriage to Helen Pitts, 47, his former secretary, caused a commotion in Washington circles.

Helen Pitts, descendant of the first white settlers of Honeoye, had first seen Douglass when she was a child and he came to the home of her abolitionist father, Gideon Pitts, who sheltered fugitive slaves in the time of the Underground.

Douglass and his new wife ignored the clamor. The bridegroom, still an impressive figure, with his mane of graying hair, a dignified beard and powerful frame, merely said: "My first wife was the color of my mother. My second wife is the color of my father."

Douglass' last national honor came in 1893 when he spoke at the Chicago World's Fair on Negro Day as commissioner from Haiti. The years had not dimmed his eloquence.

Frederick Douglass died in Washington on Feb. 20, 1895 at the age of 78. He was brought back to Rochester for burial and thousands filed past his bier as it lay in state at the City Hall. At a public service in Central Presbyterian Church the eulogy was given by Susan B. Anthony. His widow was instrumental in forming a Frederick Douglass Memorial Association. She died in 1903 and sleeps beside her husband in Mount Hope Cemetery.

On June 9, 1899, Theodore Roosevelt, Governor of New York, came to Rochester to speak at the dedication of a life-size bronze statue of Frederick Douglass in the triangle at the busy St. Paul Street-Central Avenue intersection opposite the New York Central Station. Five thousand persons marched in a parade and a small great-granddaughter of the Negro leader unveiled the monument. It had been erected through public subscription. Few cities have ever paid such a tribute to a Negro.

For 42 years the memorial stood in its downtown site. In 1941 the monument was moved to Highland Park overlooking the Bowl where outdoor operas, concerts and music festivals are held. It is near the site of the house where Douglass lived when old John Brown came to visit him.

Every year, on a date on or near the anniversary of the dedication of the monument, men and women of Frederick Douglass' race make a pilgrimage to the park and lay wreaths

51

at the feet of their foremost champion in their hour of crisis, the great orator who had been born a slave.

* * *

Harriet Tubman wasn't much to look at. She was as black as a chunk of anthracite, her upper front teeth were gone and she was only five feet tall, with the muscles of a lumberjack.

Yet she was a magnificent figure in a stormy time, an intrepid liberator. They called her the Moses and the Joan of Arc of her people. Like the plumed helmet of a medieval knight, the red bandana she wore over her short, kinky hair became the oriflamme of a crusade.

Harriet Tubman personally led out of bondage, with only the North Star as her guide, more than 300 slaves. She made raid after raid on the plantations of her native region and never was caught, although slaveholders kept raising the price on her head. When the war came, she led soldiers in battle. She served as an effective spy for the Union and as an Army nurse.

Born in a slave cabin, she could neither read nor write. Yet she was to share public platforms with the liberal intellectuals of the North and be entertained in their homes. She did not have Fred Douglass' logical mind nor his capacity for rationalization. There was not a drop of white blood in her.

As one of the chief conductors of the Underground Railway, it was her boast that "she nebber run de train off de track or lose a passenger." No cause had a more selfless leader. She had the heart of a lion and she knew no fear. As long as she lived—and that was 92 years—she never wavered in her zeal, first to liberate her people, and then to sustain them as freemen.

For more than half a century she called the Finger Lakes city of Auburn home although her cause took her to far places. The little house on the outskirts of Auburn where she lived and worked for her people is still a shrine to them.

Harriet was born in 1820 in Dorchester County on Maryland's Eastern Shore. She belonged to a planter who owned so many slaves that he hired out to others those he could not use. Her ancestors were brought to America from Africa early in the 18th Century. Her parents were slaves and as a child she lived with them in a shack on the plantation. She was variously called Araminta and Harriet Ross and finally settled on Harriet.

From early childhood she was a rebel. In later years she said the only kindness she knew came from her parents. Her mistress lashed her at the age of five because she was slow to master the details of house work. She was banished from "the Big House" to the fields, which was to her liking for she loved the outdoors.

At the age of seven she ran away after being caught stealing a lump of sugar and hid in a pig pen for five days before she returned—to suffer a sound flogging.

When she was 12, she was doing a man's work, splitting rails, hauling wood, toiling in the fields. Her arms grew powerful, her hands calloused and the sullen resentment mounted in her heavy-lidded eyes. Denied any semblance of schooling, she committed Bible verses to memory and when a hunt went on for runaway slaves, she prayed fervently for their safety.

In her teens she nearly paid for her independence of spirit with her life. After she refused to help an overseer tie up a slave who had deserted his job, the white man hurled an iron weight at the girl. It struck her on the head and for months she lay between life and death. After she recovered she was subject to spells of stupor, like a sleeping sickness, the rest of her life and she carried a scar on her head to the grave.

Her hatred of slavery and her craving for freedom grew as she heard tales of Nat Turner's slave insurrection in Virginia and learned that many Negroes were "crossing the line" to freedom through a mysterious channel known as "the Underground."

At the age of 25, she married John Tubman, a free Negro. The marriage was not a success. The light-hearted Tubman had no sympathy with her ideas of freedom and did not want to be bothered with serious things.

After five years of marriage and fearful of being sold South, Harriet made her first escape attempt. That was in 1849. She persuaded her three brothers to flee with her but they became frightened and dragged her back with them, to her disgust.

She determined to cross the line alone. A neighbor, a white woman, helped her. She gave Harriet a paper with two names on it and told her how to get to the first house named. That turned out to be the home of a farmer who looked at the note, put Harriet in his wagon, covered with a sack, and drove to the outskirts of another town. There she was directed to another station. Traveling stealthily by night, she was on free soil in Pennsylvania in a few days. Harriet Tubman thus had her first "ride" on the Underground route she was to know so well.

She went to Philadelphia where she found work as a domestic. She made the acquaintance of William Sill, a Free Negro who was "chief brakeman" of the Underground in the city, a major station on the invisible railway. The liberty-loving Quakers always supported it heartily. Harriet familiarized herself with the Underground system, saved her money and prepared for her first trip South, to bring out members of her own family.

In December, 1830, she met her sister and two children in Baltimore, where they had been spirited by others, and escorted them to free soil. That was the least spectacular of her two score raids on the slave country. Seven years later she led her parents out of bondage and cared for them as long as they lived.

In 1851 she ventured into her home territory on the Eastern Shore, hoping to persuade her husband to escape. She found he had remarried. She collected a band of slaves and piloted them to Philadelphia. While her operations centered on Maryland, she made some sallies into the deeper South.

The Fugitive Slave Law made life hazardous for escapees in the North and Canada became a haven for hundreds with St. Catherines in Ontario a major terminus of the Underground. It housed a considerable colony of blacks and Harriet made her home there for six years, while keeping up her Southern raids.

With the new emphasis on Canada, lake ports became important in the Underground system. Rochester was a major station on the invisible railway. Harriet and her wanderers found refuge in Fred Douglass' home and printing office and in the homes of Rochester abolitionists.

There also were many stations in the interior of the state. Syracuse was a hotbed of abolitionism. At nearby Peterboro was the home of Gerrit Smith, wealthy friend of the Negro. Canandaigua was an important station and so was Auburn, also a center for the publication of anti-slavery propaganda.

Along the line the fugitives hid in cellars, chimneys, hay stacks, barns, even pig pens and in board-lined dugouts used for storing vegetables. All kinds of stratagems were employed. A system of passes and codes was evolved.

Harriet would direct her bands by night through improvising new words for old plantation tunes. Sometimes men dressed as women and vice versa. Escapees were put in wagons and covered with produce. More than once slaves escaped in carriages owned by their masters.

Harriet Tubman planned her campaigns like a military commander. And she was always in complete command, enforcing iron discipline. She told few of her plans and most of her people trusted her implicitly.

"Keep moving" was her constant cry. She spurred her charges on even when they were weary and half sick. When one man of a group of 25 became panicky and was about to run back to the plantation, she pointed a revolver at him and told him to keep moving or be shot. He kept moving.

Lest crying children imperil the party in towns, Harriet would give them paregoric and toss them into a huge ticking bag she always carried.

She evaded capture, sometimes by minutes. Once when she scented danger on the main road, she plunged into a stream up to her armpits and her people followed her without a murmur.

At another time when the slave catchers closed in on her in a railroad station, she calmly pretended to read a book. The Southerners looked at the poster on the wall of the station and one of them said, "This can't be the Tubman woman. It says here she can't read or write."

According to another tale, friends once came upon her sleeping under a sign that advertised a $12,000 reward for her capture. She would have made a great actress, for she could in a twinkling transform herself into a feeble, tottering old woman—and she often used this dodge when in a corner.

It was in Auburn in the mid 1850s that she first met William H. Seward, a former Governor then in the United States

Senate where he was a leader of the anti-slavery forces. In 1857 she decided to settle in Auburn, where lived many abolitionists and Quakers. Seward, ever her friend, provided a little house for her on South Street. Later he sold it to her on generous terms, although it was then illegal for a slave to hold property. Had Seward's action been publicized, it might have harmed him politically.

The South Street house was her home the rest of her days, although during the years of her greatest activity, she was seldom there. It was there she brought her aged parents and other kinfolk.

In the late 1850s the illiterate Harriet began addressing anti-slavery meetings in the North on invitation of the abolitionist leaders, some of them intellectuals. Even in fastidious, cultured Boston, her simple, dramatic recital of her experiences, told in her plantation idiom, fascinated her audiences.

She held domestic jobs in between her Southern raids and her speech making. Her taking from the slaveholders of some $300,000 worth of human property stirred the South and in 1859 a state convention was held in Maryland to plan action against her. In the middle of the meeting Harriet led a raid into the heart of the aroused region.

She was deeply involved in John Brown's mad scheme to free the slaves and only illness prevented her from joining him in the Harper's Ferry fiasco. Brown greatly admired her as a leader and called her "General Tubman." And Harriet the rest of her life venerated the memory of "The Old Man," as she referred to Brown. To her he was the real liberator, not Lincoln, who drew her disdain because of his slowness in emancipating the Negroes.

When the curtain rose on the Civil War in April, 1861, Harriet was in Canada. Shortly she was on the fringe of the front, inducing slaves to escape to the Union lines. After the Yankees took Port Royal, S.C. in 1862, she nursed the sick among her people there and helped set up a hospital for them.

Next she was reporting to General Hunter of the Department of the South as an espionage agent. She was put in command of nine scouts and river pilots who reconnoitered the enemy and turned in some valuable reports.

Soon more active duty came her way. In July of 1863, carrying a rifle, canteen, haversack and first aid satchel and wearing bloomers, a blue coat and hat, she guided 300 Negro soldiers into the enemy country along the Combahee River in South Carolina. That band burned vast stores and many buildings and carried off nearly 800 slaves. At this time Harriet met the soldier, Nelson Davis, who was to be her second husband. He was a powerful Negro, ten years her junior.

In May 1864, while she was home on leave, she was taken ill and the people of Auburn brought her food and delicacies. On her recovery, she went into the nursing service and became matron of the Army hospital at Fortress Monroe, on the recommendation of Secretary of State Seward. But in later years, when she tried to collect for her services, even Seward's powerful aid was futile.

Homeward bound from the war, she encountered some of the brutality she had known as a young slave. She got on the wrong train through mistake. The conductor looked at her ticket and told her to get off the train. She protested that she was entitled to the same treatment as white soldiers and the conductor tried to remove her by force. When she resisted—and she was a capable scrapper—he summoned three men to his aid and the quartet threw her into a baggage car, injuring her in the struggle.

Bruised and penniless, the black "Joan of Arc," one of the heroines of her time, came home to Auburn. She may have hoped for a tranquil life; probably she did not. Anyhow, soon the aged, the maimed, the destitute of her race were swarming at her door. She turned none of them away. She fed and nursed them and gave from her slender purse. Wealthy Auburn folk gave her money and clothes for her refugees and she found peace working in her garden and orchard.

Knowing the unpreparedness of her people in the South for their new freedom, she began raising funds for freedmen's schools and eventually was supporting two of them through her own efforts.

She was balked at collecting the $1,800 war pay due her but a friend came to her rescue. Mrs. Sarah Bradford of Geneva wrote a book, *The Life and Times of Harriet Tubman* and turned the proceeds, some $1,200, over to the Negress.

Then Harriet's cup of joy overflowed and the little house in South Street resounded to the song that had guided so many foot-sore fugitives over the road to freedom before the war:

> *"There's cider in the cellar,*
> *And the black folks, they'll have some;*
> *Must be now the kingdom coming,*
> *And the year of Jubilum."*

Soon Harriet was broke again. The revenue from the book had gone to the freedmen in the South and to the refugees at home. Penniless, she roamed the public market until the tradesmen sensed her need and filled her baskets with food, gratis.

In 1869 she married Nelson Davis in Auburn's Central

Church. The Sewards, the Osbornes and others of the elite attended, along with a horde of poor blacks.

She never recovered from the sleeping spells induced by that blow on the head from the iron hurled by the overseer and in the 1880s when she sat on the platform of a suffrage meeting in Rochester, Susan B. Anthony had to awaken her from slumber to introduce her to the audience as "The Conductor of the Underground Railroad."

It was then Harriet made her celebrated remark about never running the train off the track or losing a passenger.

In her declining years she went from house to house in Auburn, peddling the produce she and her people raised on her plot. All the time she was dreaming of a home for the aged and indigent of her race.

After her husband died in 1888, she got her first government check as the widow of a war veteran. It was for $8 a month. In the late 1890s prominent Auburn people pushed a bill through Congress giving her $20 a month the rest of her life. A South Carolina Congressman fought the measure to the bitter end.

In 1896 she bought 25 acres adjoining her home at an auction. She bid $1,450 when she did not have a dime in her purse, went to a bank and obtained a mortgage on the property. In 1903 she deeded the site, along with her home, to the African Methodist Episcopal Zion Church. Five years later the home for the aged, of which she dreamed so long, was opened.

As long as she lived, the home sheltered from 12 to 15 persons at all times. After Harriet was gone, the place was abandoned. She wisely had insisted on white directors for the home. Her people put in Negro board members. The new setup failed. But there are community centers for Negroes in several cities. Each is called the Harriet Tubman Home. Her dream came true on a splendid scale.

As age bowed and withered the "Moses" of her people, she became a legend. Booker T. Washington, the famous Negro educator, came to visit her. So did hundreds of the less prominent of her race. Queen Victoria sent her a Diamond Jubilee medal and invited her to England. Reporters and magazine writers interviewed her. Few of her comrades of the Underground were left.

On March 10, 1913 she summoned two ministers and a few friends to her bedside. The shadows were gathering fast about her. She bade her friends to strike up a song, after the preachers had prayed over her. As the strains of "Swing Low, Sweet Chariot" filtered out the door of the little house in South Street, Harriet Tubman went "home." She was 92 years old.

The Grand Army of the Republic buried her with military honors. Had she not been a soldier of the Republic?

On June 12, 1914, Booker T. Washington came to Auburn again. With other Negro leaders and prominent white Auburnians, he spoke at the dedication of a tablet to her memory. The tablet is imbedded in the wall of the Court House.

The mayor of the city proclaimed the day a civic holiday and asked citizens to display the national colors. It was the first time a white community had so honored the memory of a Negro woman.

Chapter 5

Cereal Story

With a roar like thunder that startled the settlers in the valley below, the All Healing Spring burst out of the Eastern hillside above Dansville one morning in 1796.

It carried away rocks, trees and earth and carved out a chasm one mile long and a dismal cavern called the Devil's Hole high above the young settlement named after Capt. Dan Faulkner.

Clear, icy water poured from the spring and its curative properties began to be noised about. In 1852 an ailing Rochester man, Nathaniel Bingham, drank from the spring and was enthralled alike with the pure water and the glorious view from the hill.

He visualized a successful health resort at the magic spring. It was the era of the water cure. Hydrotherapy had been introduced in Europe in 1820 by Vincent Priessenitz of Silesia who had treated himself with marked success. The new therapy combined water treatment and baths with copious drinking of pure water, exercise, diet, fresh air, mental repose and no medication.

By mid century the water cure fad had spread across the country. Avon Springs, near Dansville, was approaching its heyday as a fashionable watering place and around the sulphur waters of Clifton Springs young Dr. Henry Foster was beginning his celebrated sanitarium, still on the scene.

Bingham interested another Rochester man, Lyman Granger, in the Dansville project and within a few months a rambling, four-story frame hotel with porches across its front began to rise on the East Hill. The place was called simply "the Water Cure." It opened its doors in 1853 although the structure was not completed.

After two years of deficits, the disenchanted partners sold out. The new owners fared no better and disposed of the property to a New York doctor who operated it only a short time.

It had long been vacant, had a record of failure and was badly run down when a new proprietor took over in 1858. With the advent of Dr. James Caleb Jackson a new and golden era dawned for the water cure on the hill and the village in the valley.

Jackson was a vigorous, balding man of 47 with the beard of a prophet, a pug nose and a genial smile. He radiated charm and good humor. He was experienced in the health resort field and he was an able propagandist with progressive ideas and the pioneering spirit.

He was a native of Manlius and of New England ancestry. His father had renounced medicine for farming but wanted James to be a doctor. The boy's mother hoped he would be a missionary. The precocious lad who was proficient in Latin and Greek at the age of 13, turned out to be something of both.

At the age of 18 Jackson married the daughter of an Oswego County judge and the couple went to live on a farm at Mexico, N.Y. The young husband was not up to the heavy farm labor and he began to study medicine at home.

He joined the temperance movement and began speaking at rallies of that cause. He had a natural gift for the public platform and soon was in demand as a speaker. An anti-slavery Democrat, he was attracted to the abolitionist banner. His speeches won the attention of that rich patron of every "ism," Gerrit Smith of Peterboro, who took the struggling young man under his wing. For 10 years Jackson served the Anti-Slavery Society, the backbone of the Underground Railroad. He also edited abolitionist journals. He could write as well as talk.

In 1848 failing health caused Jackson to abandon his editorial duties and he retired to a farm near his patron's home at Peterboro. The next year found him a patient at the Glenwood Springs Sanitarium at Cuba, N.Y. operated by Dr. Silas O. Gleason. Jackson became deeply interested in hydropathy.

He joined Gleason and a Miss Theodosia Gilbert in setting up the Glen Haven Water Cure near the head of Skaneateles Lake. In 1850 Gleason sold out to the other partners and opened a sanitarium on a hill above Elmira, taking several Glen Haven patients with him.

Jackson read medical books and somehow managed to snare a diploma from the Syracuse Medical Eclectic College. The fame of Glen Haven spread after he reputedly cured a woman teacher of "brain fever" without use of drugs.

Possessed of a keen sense of publicity, Dr. Jackson staged a "hygienic festival" at Glen Haven which attracted, along with a collection of cranks, such notables as Elizabeth Cady Stanton and Amelia Bloomer of equal rights fame.

The reformers of the 1850s formed a sort of "interlocking directorate." Those interested in women's rights also espoused the temperance and anti-slavery causes, as well as diet and dress reform. Dr. Jackson marched in that allied brigade, always surefootedly. At a national "Vegetable Festival," which was graced by the presence of Horace Greeley and Susan B. Anthony, he proposed—in branch water—this toast:

"Total abstinence, women's rights and vegetarianism."

Orson S. Fowler, the Cohocton-born apostle of phrenology and the octagonal house, also was a health and food faddist. His publishing house, Fowler & Wells, put out a *Water Cure Journal*, to which Dr. Jackson contributed and which helped bring patients to Glen Haven. The home-like atmosphere of the place and the personality of Dr. Jackson won it a good following.

But after flames ravaged the main building and Jackson and Miss Gilbert's new husband differed, the doctor decided to sell his interest in Glen Haven and try a fresh start somewhere else.

The Glen Haven Cure lasted a long time. One of its later operators, Dr. W. C. Thomas, proved the health-giving properties of his resort by living to the age of 107 years. Now the only vestiges of the once popular health resort are the words, Glen Haven, spelled out in white stones on a lakeside lawn.

Dr. Jackson heard of the abandoned building on Dansville's lordly hill. He looked over the site and saw its possibilities. He leased the property for three years, with an option of buying.

On the first day of October in 1858, he landed in Dansville by stage with his family and a business associate, F. Wilson Hurd. In the small retinue that had to climb the steep hill on foot, carrying its luggage, were Jackson's son, Giles, and his adopted daughter, the remarkable Dr. Harriet Austin.

Dr. Austin, then 32, fearless and articulate, had studied water therapy and had a medical diploma. She is remembered in history as the originator of "the American Costume," the water cure version of the Bloomer outfit. Designed for

65

women patients at watering places, it consisted of baggy pants and a tunic.

This mannish costume, along with Dr. Harriet's bobbed hair, upset the villagers as she dashed through Dansville's stores buying equipment for the empty building on the hill.

Before the water cure could be reopened with a new name, Our Home on the Hillside, the little staff had to banish an accumulation of rats, flies, bats, roaches, wasps, layers of dust and festoons of cobwebs.

Anxiety and struggle marked the first few months but the doctor was so charming and the scenery so grand that by the Winter of 1858 there were 50 patients. At the end of three years the enterprise was on so firm a footing that the doctor and his associates exercised their option and purchased the property. It was again renamed, this time the Health Hygenic Institute.

Gradually the plant expanded. A dozen cottages were put up around the main building and given romantic names by the doctor. Liberty Hall, a place for recreation and dining, rose in 1864. At one period, it was said, every state in the Union was represented on the roster of 300 patients.

The regimen that Dr. James Caleb Jackson instituted on the East Hill a century ago is still generally followed there although the place passed out of the hands of the Jacksons almost 40 years ago.

Dietwise Dr. Jackson followed the principles laid down by Dr. Sylvester Graham. At a time when too many Americans were gorging themselves into glassy-eyed lassitude on rich and greasy food, patients on the Hill were eating Graham bread, fresh vegetables and fruits and drinking milk and water from the All Healing Spring.

Meat and coffee were frowned upon but the patients could have them if they insisted. Nor did women have to wear "the

American costume," although the good doctor was enthusiastic for dress reform. He was too wise to enforce strict regimentation among his paying guests. Usually he found persuasion brought compliance.

Along with the hydropathic treatments, he prescribed plenty of exercise in the fresh air, plenty of sleep and sunshine—and no drugs. He would lead patients on hikes through the picturesque hills and at the highest peak bid them to bend over and view the scenery with their heads down, between their legs.

There were concerts, lectures, musicales, games, dances and talk in Liberty Hall. There were sleigh rides and May rides in season. The doctor's witty, always highly moral, lectures were popular. He promoted cordial relations between the villagers and his patients and staff. Dansville people presented home talent plays on the Hill. The village band played for special occasions, such as Founder's Day, observed every Oct. 1. Dr. Jackson was active in village affairs and gave liberally to civic causes.

The sanitarium enhanced the cultural tone of the comely, progressive village. Also Dr. Jackson opened his health center just in time to give Dansville a needed shot of economic adrenalin. The boom induced by the Genesee Valley Canal's branch was fading. No longer did the great shipments of lumber and other produce ride the canal waters. It was the new era of the Iron Horse, but so far the railroads had bypassed Dansville. So the Jackson health resort with its sizeable payroll and buying power held the life line for the village until new industries came.

Dr. Jackson kept his propaganda mills grinding. He poured out tracts on various health subjects and for more than 30 years, until 1893, his monthly magazine, *The Laws of Life,* went to all corners of the earth. At one time it had a circulation of 10,000.

Famous feet climbed steep East Hill to visit the doctor, whose hair and beard were becoming dappled with gray, but whose eyes were as merry and his chuckle as contagious as ever. Horace Greeley came and iconcoclast Robert Dale Owen and literary light Bayard Taylor. Clara Barton came and found balm for her shattered nerves. She fell in love with Dansville and after taking the cure bought a residence near the resort. She was living there when she founded in Dansville in 1881 the first chapter of the American Red Cross. She was fond of Dr. Jackson and addressed him as "Father."

James Caleb Jackson deserves a niche in history as the father of the cold cereal breakfast food. Had he concentrated as heavily on the breakfast food business, as did Dr. John Harvey Kellogg, who copied Jackson's ideas, Dansville and not Battle Creek might have become the cereal capital of the universe.

Around 1863 Dr. Jackson produced "Granula," which was a mixture of Graham flour and water, baked into thin sheets until it was brittle. Then the concoction was ground, re-baked and ground again until it came out in much the form of the present "Grape Nuts."

Gerald Carson in his excellent book, *Cornflake Crusade,* wrote that "Granula was in Dr. Kellogg's mind when he became chief physician at the Adventist Water Cure in Battle Creek. By a line of descent which can be traced clearly, 'Granula' was the prototype for 'Grape Nuts.' "

Dr. Jackson had first experimented with this breakfast food at Glen Haven and at Dansville found the white Winter wheat of the Genesee Valley ideal for his needs.

Unlike the modern instant breakfast foods, "Granula" had

to be soaked for at least 20 minutes before it could be eaten. At first the Jacksons made the cereal at the health resort. The product was so popular that a separate company, Our Home Granula Co., was formed and a building obtained in Dansville, to be exclusively used for years for the manufacture and packaging of "Granula."

In 1883 60,000 pounds of the cereal were shipped from the plant in Main Street. Eventually the Jackson family withdrew and a local baker took over the business, operating on a small scale. By 1920 "Granula," had disappeared.

For many years a companion product was "Somo," a caffein-less substitute for coffee, which the resourceful Dr. Jackson originated to please his guests who insisted on coffee with their meals. It was the daddy of Postum and the other coffee substitutes. The Granula Company's advertising slogan was "Eat Granula. Drink Somo."

The link between Dansville and Battle Creek began in 1864 when Dr. Horatio Lay, a Seventh Day Adventist from Michigan, joined the Jackson staff after his wife had been treated and recovered her health on the Hill. Through Lay, a stream of Adventists came to take the cure. They imbibed the Jackson ideas along with the waters of the All Healing Spring. One who came was a mystical leader of the church, Ellen Gould White. After studying the Jackson regimen, she announced, in the manner of Joseph Smith, the Mormon prophet, a Divine revelation which commanded her to set up at Battle Creek, the Adventist stronghold, a duplicate of Dr. Jackson's Dansville cure. Of that vision, and largely through the genius of Adventist Dr. Kellogg, whose wife came from Alfred, there evolved at Battle Creek the world famous health and cereal center.

In 1879 Dr. J. C. Jackson, in failing health, turned over the active direction of the health center to his son, Dr. James

H., who had been general manager since 1862. The older man kept up his writing, editing and lecturing.

On the night of June 26, 1882, a kerosene lamp upset in a patient's room and flames raced through the doomed wooden main building. The staff got every one of the 150 patients out and firemen saved Liberty Hall and nearby cottages by knocking down the corridor that linked the hall with the burning building.

Dr. James H. Jackson raised $120,000 and built the present fireproof structure, which crowns the East Hill like a baronial castle. The new building was completed by Founder's Day of 1883 and the name of the resort changed to the Jackson Sanatorium. Later it was the Jackson Health Resort.

The founder made his home in North Adams, from 1886 to 1895. He still edited *The Laws of Life,* maintained a voluminous correspondence and was particularly interested in the affairs of the Republican party which he had joined at its birth. He made periodic visits to Dansville and while on one of them, died on July 11, 1895, in his 85th year.

The health center remained in the Jackson family until 1914 when it was forced into receivership. The third of the line, Dr. James Arthur Jackson, had valiantly tried to carry on in a new order.

During World War I the old water cure was a government hospital for veterans suffering from nervous disorders. After 1921 it was operated for a time by two Buffalo physicians. In 1929 it passed into the sinewy hands of the little physical culture apostle, the fantastic Bernarr MacFadden, and it got a new name, the Physical Culture Hotel. While he maintained its traditions of healthful diet and exercise, he put on spectacular stunts of which old Dr. Jackson, with all his flair for publicity, would hardly have approved.

After MacFadden's death, the property was purchased by

a New York hotel man. His guests are mainly from the metropolitan area and the Hill seems more remote from the Valley than in the old days.

There have been many changes in a century. But the view from the Eastern hill is as magnificent as it was when Dr. James Caleb Jackson had to chase out the bats and wasps before he could open his "Home on the Hillside."

The founder of that historic haven for the ailing and the weary was a pioneer, years ahead of his time in many ways.

And when you munch your breakfast toasties, corn flakes or whatever, give a thought to Dr. Jackson of Dansville, who started this whole cold cereal vogue with his "Granula" back in the time of the Civil War.

Chapter 6

"Head Man"

Orson Squire Fowler was a country boy who made good in the big city. He found gold and glory at the end of his personal rainbow because he used his head—and the heads of a lot of other people.

For this onetime Cohocton farm boy was the high priest of phrenology when it was all the rage in America, in the 1840s and 1850s. He also popularized another more lasting fad—the octagonal style of architecture.

In his rise to temporary fame and fortune Orson Fowler pulled along with him a younger brother and a sister from the Steuben County hills.

Phrenology is—or was—the "science" of rating mental faculties and traits by studying the contours of the human cranium. "By their bumps ye shall know them," was the slogan of the tribe of phrenologists whose name was legion in the heyday of the fad. And Orson Squire Fowler was the head man of the head readers.

"Bumpology," as the irreverent called it, was introduced in 1796 by Franz Joseph Gall, a Viennese brain surgeon. The Austrian government banned his lectures as inimical to religion and morals. So Gall and his pupil, Johann Sputzheim, took their teachings to France where they were more favorably received. Gall died in 1828 and Sputzheim in 1832, soon after he had begun preaching the gospel of phrenology in the United States.

Among those who heard one of his last lectures in Boston were two young theological students, classmates at Amherst College. Both were much impressed. One of them was Orson Fowler, a lean, keen, energetic chap with piercing blue eyes. The other was Henry Ward Beecher, broad shouldered, virile, magnetic, with a gift of gab.

Beecher was a native of Litchfield, Conn., the son of Lyman Beecher, a renowned Congregationalist divine who sired an illustrious brood. Fowler was born in Cohocton in 1809, three years after his parents had left Vermont for the Steuben County frontier. His father was a founder and a deacon of the Cohocton Congregational Church.

Orson was the oldest of three children. Lorenzo Niles was born in 1811 and Charlotte in 1814. The Fowlers, while far from wealthy, were not destitute. In his youth Orson worked on the farm and attended the local schools. At the age of 16 he joined the Congregational Church and his parents hoped he would become a minister. With that career in view, he enrolled at Amherst in 1830. For two years he paid his own way by doing carpenter work and odd jobs.

After he and his chum, Beecher, had heard Sputzheim explain the tenets of phrenology, they read every book and tract on the subject they could lay their hands on. They became so versed in "bumpology" that Beecher began speaking to scientific groups on the campus while Fowler "read" their fellow-students' heads at two cents per skull. Then each student was told the vocation for which he was best fitted, as indicated by the bumps.

The partners were so encouraged by their success that they began putting on their act in nearby Massachusetts towns. Beecher's golden tongue and Fowler's nimble hands brought in the dollars and the golden flood made the Yankee blood of the young phrenologists dance.

But at graduation time their paths parted. Beecher determined his destiny lay in the pulpit and he became the most famous preacher of his time. One wonders if Fowler ever explored his friend's cranium and discovered the "bump of amativeness," a trait so sensationally revealed in Henry Ward Beecher's later years.

But Orson Fowler believed the new field of phrenology offered more promise than preaching the Gospel. In 1836 he opened an office in New York as a practicing phrenologist. He was pioneering. Brother Lorenzo quit his studies at Amherst to join him. As the phrenology craze spread, they wrote books on the subject and lectured extensively.

They did so well that in 1837 sister Charlotte came on from Cohocton to help her brothers. That same year Samuel R. Wells, a Connecticut Yankee who had lived in Western New York, took over the management of the publishing end of the business—and married Charlotte.

The Fowlers were the bellwethers of the phrenology flock but they could not keep rivals out of the flourishing business. In the 1840s men in long tailed coats were popping up all over the country, giving their sales talks and reading heads and character—for a price.

Orson Squire Fowler, the high priest of the cult, was never at rest. When he was not writing books and reading heads, he was lecturing. When he came to Prattsburg, near his birthplace, he insisted on being blindfolded when he did his head reading because, he said, "I know the subjects too well."

Books and tracts poured from his pen, to be printed and distributed by Fowler & Wells. His *Fowler's Self Instructor* was sold by the itinerant phrenologists at their meetings, along with written charts of the buyers' characteristics. A best seller was Fowler's *Practical Phrenology*, which in the 1840s and 1850s had its place on thousands of parlor tables, along with The Word and *Paradise Lost*.

Fowler and the other phrenologists divided the skull into purely arbitrary regions, the size of each denoting the faculty resident there. The prominences and depressions revealed the mental powers and traits of character.

A formidable array of faculties were listed, including the mouth-filling word, Philoprogenitiveness (parental love), adhesiveness (social feeling), vitaviviness (love of existence as such), alimentativeness (appetite for sustenance), casuality (power of reasoning). The head readers disdained the use of simple terms. They bedazzled the public with their pompous jargon.

Fowler wrote a book on memory 70 years before "Addison Sims of Seattle." He wrote a series of books giving advice on sex relations, much like the later works of the learned Dr. Stall, author of *What A Young Man Should Know*, *What A Young Woman Should Know* and other guides to human behavior.

True to his pious upbringing, Orson Fowler deplored the use of intoxicants, tight lacing by the ladies and theater going.

He assailed "life-killing" drugs and exhorted physicians to inform the people how to preserve their health, instead of confining themselves to the cure of disease. In preaching preventive medicine, he was years ahead of his time. He maintained that if humans would follow simple rules of health and hygiene, they would not need pills and nostrums. He called the eating of "animal meat" and coffee drinking injurious to health.

Fowler's books sold by the thousands, especially those dealing with the human emotions. The author was to have experience aplenty in the realm of love and marriage. In his lifetime he married thrice. His first wife was a member of an old New York family. After she died, he married again in 1865 and soon after the demise of his second spouse, he took as his third bride a spinster of 43. That was in 1882 when he was 73 years old. She bore him three children.

Lorenzo's wife, Lydia Folger, was active in the phrenology field and in various reform movements. She had received from Syracuse Central Medical College the second medical degree granted a woman in the United States.

In its heyday phrenology won some notable converts, among them Walt Whitman, the poet, and Horace Greeley, the editor, who embraced every new "ism." Orson opened a branch office in Washington where statesmen came to have their characters analyzed and plaster busts made. The latter was a profitable sideline. There was some guile attached to the snare of this Fowler. He never reported finding any undesirable traits in his study of the heads of his important clients. To his credit, he never descended to fortune telling or forecasting of future events.

The dollars rolled in from the books and the lectures. In 1855 Orson and Lorenzo sold their interests in the publishing house to Wells, Charlotte's husband, who ran it until his death in 1875. After that his widow, a woman of parts, headed Fowler & Wells until the firm was sold in 1895. By that time phrenology was long out of date.

Orson and Lorenzo, bearded like prophets of old, continued their lecture tours, their writing and office practice. The home of the Lorenzo Fowlers in New York became a salon for advanced thinkers. Among their guests were Mrs. Amelia Bloomer, the Seneca Falls editor for whom the celebrate suffragist costume was named, and her fellow crusader, Susan B. Anthony. Both these ladies appeared in trousers at a women's rights meeting over which Lydia Fowler presided—in conventional attire.

In 1860 Lorenzo and Lydia made a lecture tour of England. It was so successful that they remained in London for the rest of their lives.

In the late 1840s Orson Fowler somehow found time to ride a new hobby and to make it a national fad. Impressed by an eight-sided house in Jaynesville, Wis., known locally as "Goodrich's Folly," he became a disciple of the octagonal style of architecture. It was by no means new. There were eight-sided buildings in Italy in the Middle Ages. As early as 1813 there was an octagonal house in Richmond, Vt. Fowler apparently did not know there were a few already built in his native Western New York when he began beating his drum for the "octagon."

He gave the style nation-wide publicity through a book, *A Home for All or the Gravel Wall and Octagonal Mode of Building*, which came out in 1849. He described the walls of the Wisconsin house which were built of a combination of lime, small stones and sand (grout) and cited among the advantages of the eight-sided building: Conservation of heat and also of light, by providing more sunlight during the daylight hours. He also claimed the octagonal style saved the housewife many steps.

The distinctiveness of the design and the prestige of Orson Fowler combined to popularize the "octagons" and soon eight-sided houses, in addition to barns, stores, schoolhouses and churches were dotting the American landscape.

The father of the fad built the most pretentious and widely publicized of all the "octagons." Fowler's fantastic mansion began to rise on a knoll just North of Fishkill on the Albany Post Road in 1849 and it was not completed until 1858.

It had four stories, 100 rooms and a basement. An inside

toilet was a sensation. Crowning the monstrous structure was a glass-roofed cupola which towered 80 feet above the ground. The house was ringed with porches connected by outside stairways.

"Fowler's Folly" became the showplace of the Hudson region. People flocked from far and near to see the great house and have the great phrenologist read their heads. So many came for Fowler's lectures that he had to convert four rooms of his house into an auditorium.

He was riding the crest of popularity when tragedy struck the eight-sided house on the knoll. Seepage from a cesspool carried typhoid germs through the highly touted but impractical grout walls and several died of the fever.

The Fowlers fled the place, which became a white elephant. For a time it housed a military school, then a boarding house. It changed hands 30 times, each time for less money, before it was abandoned to the rats and the spiders. Finally it was ordered razed in 1897. It was a hazard to the visitors who still flocked to "Fowler's Folly."

The fortunes of "the professor" with the bright blue eyes and the patriarchal beard sank in his later years. From 1863 to 1880 he lived at Manchester, Mass. He did some lecturing and wrote books, in the same vein as in the lush years. But few attended his lectures and his books did not sell.

Phrenology was only a fad and it went the way of all fads. Its heyday ended with the outbreak of the Civil War. A new generation scoffed at "bumpology." A skeptic was heard to remark: "Maybe that 'bump of sublimity' the phrenologist made so much of was the result of a boyhood fall from an apple tree."

Death came to Orson Squire Fowler in 1887 in Sharon Springs, N.Y. He had caught a chill while working on his little farm. He had lived 78 exciting years.

The chief apostle of phrenology, "the head man of the head readers," lived to see that fad fade away but the other craze he popularized lives on today in the hundreds of octagonal buildings still standing in every corner of the land.

Chapter 7

The Sisters and the Spirits

Hardly had the Fox family moved into the little house at the crossroads than they began hearing the queer noises in the night.

There were uncanny knockings in the bedroom and in the cellar. There were noises like that of a heavy object falling and being dragged down the cellar stairs, followed by a sound like shoveling.

When the year 1848 dawned there were four Foxes living in the story and a half frame house at Hydesville, a hamlet just north of the canal town of Newark: John Fox, a blacksmith; Margaret, his wife, and their two younger daughters, Margaret, 15, and Katherine, 12. A son, David, lived on a farm nearby and a widowed daughter, Leah Fish, in her early 30s, gave music lessons in her home on Mechanics Square (now Madison Park South) in Rochester.

They were natives of Canada who had moved from Bath in Ontario to Rochester in 1844. In Rochester they lived in Charlotte and later on Plymouth Avenue. They moved into the Hydesville house in December of 1847 after a brief residence in Newark.

The Foxes were Methodists and bore a good reputation, although, it was said, John Fox in his younger days had been a drinking man. His two most famous daughters in maturity were to become familiar with spirits other than those they invoked from the other world.

John Fox was of German descent and the family name originally had been Voss. His wife, born Margaret Routan, was of French lineage and had a strain of mysticism in her makeup. Some of her ancestors were said to have possessed "second sight."

The Foxes heard the talk in the neighborhood that their new home at Hydesville was "haunted," although most of the grisly tales about "the Spook House" came out after it became famous. Then, it seemed, memories were suddenly refreshed. Stolid John Fox apparently paid little heed to these tales, but his superstitious wife and two impressionable little girls drank them in.

Lucretia Pulver, who had lived in the house in 1843-44 as the hired girl of John Bell, told of knockings in the bedroom and ghostly footfalls about the house. A later tenant, Michael Weekman, who lived there for a year and a half before the Foxes, said he had heard loud raps at his door and found no one there when he answered them. He also claimed his eight-year-old daughter had felt a cold hand on her cheek at night.

Early in 1848 the mysterious noises began to plague the Fox family and rob them of their sleep. There were rappings and jarrings and scraping sounds and the young girls told of waking to feel a clammy hand on their faces and sometimes the touch of a dog's paw.

Late in March the noises became so intense and so frequent that Fox searched the house of nights with a lighted candle but found nothing. On March 30 the uncanny rappings continued through most of the night.

The weary parents hoped to get some sleep the next night but early in the evening there came an almost continuous outbreak of inexplicable noises. The girls, who slept in the bedroom with their parents, were all agog.

History was made when Katie playfully snapped her fingers three times and called out: "Hey, Mr. Splitfoot, do as I do." Out of the nowhere came "Mr. Splitfoot's" instant answer —three loud, distinct raps.

Not to be outdone, sister Margaret got into the act by clapping her hands and directing: "No, do just as I do. Count one, two, three, four." Four raps sounded in response.

Katie then made a certain number of motions with her fingers—noiselessly. From the invisible came the same number of raps. The girl turned to her wide-eyed mother, saying, "See, mother, he can see as well as hear."

Mrs. Fox took a hand in the game by asking the number of her children and their ages. The correct answers were rapped out. When she asked, "Are you a man?" no answer came, but to the question, "Are you a spirit?" a rap sounded.

Mrs. Fox had a neighbor, Mrs. Redfield, called in and the "spirit" answered her questions.

Thus on the last night of the madcap month in March in 1848 in a humble home modern Spiritualism was born. For the children's "Mr. Splitfoot" became identified as a disembodied spirit and the "conversation" of that night was declared to be the first communication in all history between this world and the next.

In that same mystical countryside, shadowed by the drumlins, those strange-shaped hillocks that are relics of the Ice Age, two decades earlier a shambling farm youth named Joseph Smith had conversed with angels and the Mormon Church had been born.

* * *

Word of the strange goings-on in the Fox house spread

and more and more neighbors flocked there to listen to the rappings. They noted that their questions were answered only in the presence of Margaret and Katie. Among them a simple code was evolved by numbering the letters of the alphabet.

By this method, the spirit revealed that in life he had been Charles B. Rosna, a 31-year-old peddler with a wife and five children, who had been murdered in that house five years before. His throat had been cut with a butcher knife, $500 had been taken from his pockets and he was lugged down to the cellar where he was buried in a grave 10 feet deep. The time given for the murder occurred during the two days the hired girl had been sent away from the house. It was on her return, she said, that she heard the gruesome noises.

Fox and several neighbors began digging in the cellar but had to abandon the search when water was struck at three feet. In the Summer the digging was resumed and was rewarded with the finding of some bones and hair, said to have belonged to a human skeleton, along with evidences of quick lime and charcoal.

It is noteworthy that no such person as Charles B. Rosna had ever been heard of in the neighborhood and that the sudden disappearance of the father of five children passed unnoticed at the time of his supposed murder.

Meanwhile, in the Spring of 1848, the spirits became more active. On April 2 the raps were heard in the daytime for the first time. The house seemed to sway with the violence of the knockings, furniture moved and cold hands snatched the bedclothes from the little girls at night—or so they said.

These new manifestations brought swarms of curious people to the house. Five hundred came in a single day. The blacksmith and his wife were deeply disturbed. It is said Mrs. Fox's hair turned white within a week. The little girls did not seem to mind the attention they got. But some neighbors began making unkind remarks about the "Spook House," as they called it. The Foxes moved into the home of the son, David.

The local newspapers played up the "spirit talks." In Rochester Leah Fox Fish read about them and hurried to Wayne County as fast as canal packet could carry her. She took her mother and Katie home with her.

But separating the sisters did not end the knockings. They startled passengers on the Rochester-bound canal boat. They sounded in the home of David. They persisted in the home of Leah, even after she had moved into the half of a double house on Prospect Street. The occupants of the other half swore out eviction papers. The whole family was reunited in a new abode on the south side of Troup Street, in the then fashionable Third Ward. The frame house, once the home of Deacon Alvah Strong, still stands at 107½ Troup, back from the street.

As people began gathering there to "talk with the spirits," Leah's keen business sense asserted itself and she conceived the idea of charging a small fee. Thus began the first professional seances in America. Prominent among the early converts were Isaac and Amy Post, leaders in the abolition movement.

At Hydesville only the spirit of the slain peddler was invoked by Margaret and Katherine. In the Rochester seances it was discovered that many other disembodied spirits could be induced to speak to the girls.

Word of this psychic phenomena spread throughout Rochester and Leah heeded "a command" from the spirits to hold public demonstrations. The well-rounded Mrs. Fish, who was soon to become Mrs. Brown and later Mrs. Underhill, had a talent for management. Two other promoters appeared in E. W. Capron of Auburn and George Willetts of Rochester. Corinthian Hall, Rochester's large new meeting place, was selected as the site, Nov. 14 as the date and 25 cents a head as the admission fee to be charged.

Corinthian Hall was filled with a curious and none too friendly crowd of 400 when Margaret appeared on the stage, with Leah at her side. Katie was out of town. After the hall was filled with knockings, the audience named a committee of five to investigate and report the next evening. The committee subjected Margaret and Leah to several tests and reported it could not discover the cause of the rappings nor did it find any evidence of deceit.

A second committee, that included the eminent Vice Chancellor Frederick Whittelsey, was appointed, investigated and made the same report as the first. Public opinion, notably among church people, was aroused and when at another meeting, a third committee submitted another inconclusive report, a mob rushed for the stage where sat the Fox sisters. It was driven back by the city police justice, Samuel Moore, and a squad of picked men.

That mob scene was a press agent's dream come true. Newspapers all over the country played up the "Rochester Rappings." A new church was taking form.

In Rochester the seances became more frequent and better attended. Leah discovered that she, too, possessed occult powers and went into the medium business along with her sisters.

Dr. Augustus H. Strong, Rochester theologian, in his "Reminiscences of Early Rochester," gave this account of a seance he attended as a youth in the Troup Street house:

"That was a memorable evening for me. It began very solemnly with the wheeling out of a heavy mahogany center table into the middle of the parlor. Then the company

85

gathered tremblingly around it and formed a closed circle by clasping hands about its edges. Then we waited in silence.

"Katie Fox was opposite me. I thought I observed a slight smile upon her face. I was less observant of the proprieties at the time than I have been since, and I ventured to wink at Katie Fox. And I thought that Katie did something like winking in return. She was a pretty girl and why shouldn't she? But soon she composed her countenance.

"The seance proceeded solemnly to the end. But for me there was no more solemnity or mystery . . . there was no manner of doubt about the rappings. These began under the table. Then they seemed to proceed from the floor. At last they came from the doors of the room and even from the ceiling. Questions were proposed to the so-called spirits, and ambiguous or commonplace answers were spelled out. I do not remember a single question that gave knowledge of any value or beyond what the questioners already possessed."

Doctor Strong wrote of the investigation into the knockings made by Miss Mary B. Allen, preceptress of a school for young ladies which Katie Fox had at one time attended. Miss Allen asked to communicate with the spirit of her grandmother and posed the question: "How does my grandmother now spell the word 'scissors'?" When the spirit of her grandma spelled out "sissers," the amused Miss Allen said:

"Oh, that is just the way Katie Fox spelled the word when she was a scholar at my school."

Medical science took a dim view of the manifestations. Three members of the University of Buffalo Medical School faculty gave the Fox sisters a series of tests. The doctors reported that no raps were forthcoming when the sisters' feet were placed in separate chairs in front of them and their knees held firmly. The conclusion was—the raps were produced by the girls snapping their knee joints. As simple as that.

Despite the skeptics and all the investigations, Spiritualism had caught the popular imagination and was gaining momentum as a new half century began. Spirit circles were organized and new mediums popped up all over the land.

In 1850 the spirits evidently told the Foxes to spread their wings and their gospel beyond the limits of Rochester where they had first achieved national notoriety. They went on tour of Albany, Troy and other Upstate cities and July 1 found them in the metropolis of New York. There the spotlight beat upon them fiercely indeed.

Leah and Mrs. Fox accompanied the young girls on their invasion of the Big Town. Seances there were attended by such notables as James Fenimore Cooper, William Cullen Bryant, John Bigelow, historian George Bancroft, N. P. Willis, the poet-dandy, and Horace Greeley, editor of the *Tribune*.

A dozen of these learned gentlemen gave out a guarded statement, in which they admitted that the girls—or the spirits—gave them the correct answers but they disavowed any belief that there had been any communication with the departed.

Greeley, an eager champion of most every new idea, strongly defended the sisters and Spiritualism. He wrote in his newspaper:

"Whatever may be the origin or cause of the rappings, the ladies in whose presence they occur do not make them. We tested them thoroughly and to our entire satisfaction."

The editor entertained the Foxes for a week in his home and his ailing wife became a convert. Later "Uncle Horace" became bored with his new fad, for he commented:

"To sit for two dreary mortal hours in a darkened room in

87

a mixed company, waiting for someone's disembodied grand-mother or aunt to tip tables or reopen a door is dull music at best."

Greeley's rival, James Gordon Bennett of the *Herald* made a vitriolic attack on the Foxes and the learned men who witnessed their demonstration, declaring that: "A dozen of the Herald's newsboys would have detected the fraud within five minutes, but the ventriloquists of the Rochester knockings have successfully humbugged the twelve great philosophers."

The country girls had really arrived—when two great editors battled over them. The Foxes spent a lucrative nine weeks in New York before returning to Rochester, where they had a new abode in a part of the pillared mansion at the northwest corner of Plymouth Avenue and Troup Street.

In 1851 the tribe moved to New York where spectacular careers lay ahead for Maggie and Katie, with manager Leah in the wings.

As they began holding meetings and seances in New York, the Fox sisters became the acknowledged high priestesses of a rapidly growing cult. By 1852 there were 2,000 mediums in the United States and many in other lands.

In the flesh the sisters of the spirit were comely, slender and well-formed, with regular features. Margaret, although capable of intense feeling, was milder mannered and more the pensive type than her roguish younger sister. Maggie was dark-eyed and brown haired. Katie was remembered for her large, luminous gray eyes. She wore her soft brown hair in braids that hung down to her waist. She affected a plainness of style in dress. But there was always something pert and elfin about Katie Fox.

Both girls were to have their affairs of the heart. Margaret's romance came in 1852, in the City of Brotherly Love.

Bloomer Girls Elizabeth Cady Stanton, left, and Amelia Bloomer.

Elizabeth Blackwell, "First Lady Doctor" and old Geneva College.

She and her mother had gone to Philadelphia for meetings and seances and at a reception met a social lion, Dr. Elisha Kent Kane, explorer-scientist, recently returned from his Arctic expedition in relief of Sir John Franklin.

This sophisticated celebrity of 33 years fell madly in love with the 18-year-old country girl who talked with spirits. He vowed she would be his. Kane's wealthy family tried to end the attachment. So did Leah who saw the flow of gold from Margaret's mediumship stopped. For Kane wanted his beloved to drop all connection with Spiritualism.

The love affair was not broken off. Kane put the girl in a fashionable school while he departed on another Arctic journey. Before he left, he had a celebrated Italian artist paint Margaret and he carried her likeness with him into the frozen wastes.

Kane's health began to fail. His physician ordered him to rest in a warmer clime. Before he left for Cuba, he and Margaret were married in a Quaker ceremony, in the presences of her mother, Katie, a young woman caller and a servant. The unorthodox marriage was to be kept secret until his return.

But the doctor never returned. He died in Havana on Feb. 16, 1857, a few days before Margaret and her mother were to have joined him. He willed Margaret income from a trust fund but it was in his brother's name. The brother refused to recognize the marriage or to make any payments.

After Margaret had been driven to the courts, a compromise settlement was effected, with the Kane family agreeing to pay the interest on the fund and to give Margaret $2,000 in cash. But the Kanes reneged on the compact and Margaret never realized enough from the estate to pay her lawyers.

She had loved her explorer dearly and went into deep mourning for 14 years, giving up all spirit rappings. She also joined the Catholic Church as her lover had desired. In 1865, which was the year both her inconspicuous father and her ubiquitous mother died, she put out a book under the titilating title of "The Love Life of Doctor Kane." It contained his letters to her and her version of the squabble.

In the meantime Katie, under the management of Leah, who was now Mrs. Underhill (her third husband was a well-to-do New Yorker), was doing very well in the Big Town. From 1861 to 1866 her professional services belonged exclusively to banker Charles F. Livermore, for whom she gave nearly 400 sittings. Livermore was generous and Katie had money for travel. She sailed for England in 1871. There she held seances and married a barrister named Henry D. Jencken. She bore him two sons. Jencken died in 1881 and his widow returned to the United States, after a visit to Russia.

In 1876 need of money drove Margaret back into the world of seances and spirits. She became the high priestess of a "Spiritual Mansion," maintained by rich Henry Seybert of Philadelphia. There she reportedly communicated with the Apostles and the angel Gabriel.

Seybert set up a chair of psychic research at the University of Pennsylvania. Out of that grew a commission to study Spiritualism. Margaret Fox Kane was the first subject of investigation. In 1884 the commission's report branded her an unmitigated fraud.

In New York the widowed Katie was having her troubles. A welfare society obtained a court order, taking her two children away from her, alleging ill treatment and citing her intemperance. Later she recovered their custody.

The two sisters were addicted to drink in this period of their careers. Leah broke with Margaret because she did not like the latter's way of life but she stuck with Katherine—

until 1888 when the two younger Fox sisters stormed back into the headlines.

There appeared in the *New York Herald* on Sept. 24, 1888, a story telling of an impending "interesting exposure of fraud" by Margaret Fox. This threat sent dismayed leaders of Spiritualism to the firing line with charges that Margaret was either out of her mind or under the influence of liquor —or both. In October the blow they dreaded struck, in the form of a full-page spread in the *New York World* under the heading:

"A DREADFUL LIFE OF DECEPTION"

Asserting that she had long wanted to expose Spiritualism as "a fraud of the worst deception," she explained the cause of the famous rappings:

"The rappings are simply the result of a perfect control of the muscles of the leg below the knee which govern the tendons of the foot and allow action of the toe and ankle bones that are not commonly known. Such perfect control is only possible when a child is taken at an early age and carefully and continually taught to practice the muscles which grow stiff in later years. . . . With control of the muscles of the foot, the toes may be brought down to the floor without any movement that is perceptible to the eye. The whole foot, in fact, can be made to give rappings by the use only of muscles below the knee. This, then, is the simple explanation of the whole method of knocks and raps."

She added that "I know there is no such thing as the departed returning to this life. I have tried to do so in every form and know that it cannot be done."

Then she described how she and Katie when they were little girls in Hydesville concocted the rappings to frighten their gullible mother:

"My sister Katie and myself were very young children when this horrible deception began. . . . We were very mischievous children, and we wanted to terrify our dear mother, who was a very good woman and easily frightened. At night, when we went to bed, we used to tie an apple to a string and move the string up and down, making a strange noise every time it would rebound. Mother listened to this for a time. She could not understand it and did not suspect us of being capable of a trick because we were so young.

"At last she could stand it no longer and she called the neighbors in and told them about it. It was this that set us to discover the means of making the raps. I think, when I reflect about it, that it was a most wonderful discovery—and all through our mischief. . . . As to the thought of spirits, this never entered our brains."

A few nights after this bombshell burst, Margaret appeared on the stage of the crowded Academy of Music in Brooklyn. Katherine, who backed up her sister in every particular of the confession, was in a box. Leah now was hostile to both sisters.

When she came to speak, Margaret found herself tongue-tied. Rabid Spiritualists maintained she was under the influence of liquor, but others of the faith conceded that she was sober.

It did not matter. Her toe-joint spoke for her—and eloquently. A wooden stool with four legs was put in front of her. Baring her right foot, she placed it on the stool which acted as a sounding board. Then the hushed crowd heard a number of sharp raps—the same mysterious sounds that had electrified the neighbors in Hydesville so many years ago.

A committee of physicians who watched the proceedings carefully and examined the foot agreed that "the sounds were made by the action of her large toe."

Spiritualism may have reeled momentarily from this blow but in 1889 the church was on too firm a foundation and had too many followers to be wrecked by any "confession."

And the next year it recovered completely when Margaret repudiated her confession as entirely false. She said she had been induced to undermine Spiritualism by "persons high in the Roman Catholic Church."

In the tempest that followed Margaret's turn-about, it was charged that she had been paid both for the expose and for the recantation. Katie, not then hard pressed for funds, never repudiated her sister's story of the origin of the rappings.

Within a few years all the sisters were at rest—in that other world which in their lifetimes they had tried to explore. Leah Fox-Fish-Brown Underhill died in 1890; Katherine, who late in life had married a New Yorker named Sparr, died in penury in 1892 and Margaret followed her the next year. The two younger sisters are buried in Cypress Hills, Brooklyn.

The girls from Hydesville had gone far. On their way up, they had faced mobs, ridicule and dissension. Their lives were not saintly but they had carved their names in the saga of America.

It seems well nigh incredible that a world-wide religion could have sprung from such beginnings as the rappings in the night. Yet the times were ripe. It was the heyday of the isms—mesmerism, animal magnetism, clairvoyance, electro-biology, hydrotherapy, Mormonism, Millerism, Fourierism, phrenology.

From the dawn of time the question of man's immortality had challenged the human mind. Attempts to communicate with the land beyond the grave had been made in many lands and in many centuries before the playful Fox girls strode on the occult stage.

The doctrines of the Swedish savant, Swedenborg, had many adherents in colonial America. The rappings, which became the trademark of the sisters Fox, were by no means unheard of. Mysterious knockings had been reported in Germany in 1520 and in England in 1661 and 1716. In 1825 in Wurttemberg, Germany, a woman told of nightly visits by a male apparition whose coming was always announced by knockings. Three years before the Hydesville manifestations, an Ohio girl, mesmerized by her father, presented in pantomime the mannerisms of deceased relatives.

But it was in the blacksmith's cottage at Hydesville in 1848 that the inexplicable noises were given a meaning and contact established with the spirits for the first time.

Out of the Western New York rappings evolved the many facets of Spiritualism and the many types of mediums—the rappers, the table tilters, those who spoke the words of the spirits, those who wrote down the messages, the trance and levitation experts and the rest.

The cult, which became unified as a church after the Civil War, won some notable converts, other than Horace Greeley, whose enthusiasms were often transitory. Among them were the Utopian, Robert Dale Owen, son of a famous father; John Worth Edmonds, a judge of the New York State Court of Appeals, who became a medium and a writer on Spiritualism; former Governor Tallmadge of Wisconsin. And in later years, in England, there were such notables as Sir A. Conan Doyle, the creator of the immortal Sherlock Holmes, and Oliver Lodge.

Learned men have lectured and written about Spiritualism. One who was not learned but was an expert on his subject, P. T. Barnum, in his book, *Humbugs of the World,* devoted a chapter to the cult. Many years later in another book, *A Magician among the Spirits,* Harry Houdini wrote devastatingly of Spiritualistic claims and of the Fox rappings.

Spiritualists were gleeful in November of 1904 when the world was told of the finding of the skeleton of a man in the walls of the Hydesville house where 56 years earlier the Fox girls had invoked the spirit of the slain peddler.

School children playing in the deserted "Spook House" came upon the bones between the earth and the crumbling cellar wall. Along with the skeleton was found a tin trunk such as used by peddlers in the early days.

Skeptics were quick to point out that the spirit had located the body buried deep in the center of the cellar, not in its walls, but Spiritualists hailed the discovery as positive vindication of the Fox sisters and the claims of the church.

Conan Doyle declared: "These discoveries settle the question forever and prove conclusively that a crime *was* committed in this house and that the crime was indicated by psychic means."

In 1916 Benjamin F. Bartlett of Cambridge Springs, Pa., purchased the Fox house from the Hyde family and had it moved from Hydesville to Lily Dale, a world shrine of Spiritualism. In that colony, established in 1887, amid the rolling Chautauqua hills beside four pretty little lakes, the historic house was reconstructed and set up in the "Forest Grove." There thousands have viewed the birthplace of modern Spiritualism and gazed at a peddler's tin trunk, one of the most prized exhibits.

In that house a noted medium, Flo Cottrell of Holland, N.Y. held seances and reproduced the rappings heard in the old building in 1848. In September, 1955, flames devoured the "Spook House" that was a shrine to so many Spiritualists.

For half a century the "mother church" was in Rochester,

in Plymouth Avenue South opposite the last home of the Fox family in that city. In 1906 the Spiritualists took over the abandoned Plymouth Congregational Church, a stately brick edifice with a tall spire.

There state and national assemblies of the church were held and noted mediums gave demonstrations. On Dec. 3, 1927, a 21-foot high plain white granite shaft commemorating the founding of Spiritualism in Western New York was unveiled on the church lawn. The memorial was suggested by Conan Doyle during a lecture tour in Upstate New York and he gave liberally to the fund that erected it. In 1955 the century-old church was razed to make way for Rochester's Inner Loop and the monument was moved to a more conspicuous site nearby.

After the Fox cottage was moved to Lily Dale, the historic Hydesville site was neglected. Weeds grew over the plot at the corner of Hydesville and Parker Roads and fallen trees lay where they fell. Finally an automobile graveyard took over.

In 1927 Mrs. M. E. Cadwallader, a Spiritualist leader, had a stone marker placed on the site of the birthplace of the church. And in 1948, on the 100th anniversary of the first rappings, the Fox Memorial Society, which had acquired 146 acres at Hydesville, dedicated a large converted barn to be used for housing pilgrims to the shrine. A stone memorial chapel was built, the plot was landscaped and every year many of the faithful visited the historic crossroads in the shadow of the drumlins.

One September night in 1954, flames destroyed the hotel. Recently, a dining hall, which adjoins a new motel operated by a Spiritualist woman minister, was built on the site. The little stone chapel, called "The Healing Shrine," still stands on the hillside, beside "The Wishing Well," which welcomes contributions.

In the field in the rear of the site of the Fox house there are some concrete blocks, the beginnings of the wall of a building which never was completed. On the wall facing the Hydesville Road is a plaque, which tells that here is a shrine dedicated to "every gifted medium from the time of the Fox sisters." That cornerstone was laid in 1955. Today that's all there is of the shrine.

But beside the road, on the site of the cottage where the young Fox girls first talked with "Mr. Splitfoot" so many years ago, the marker stands, proclaiming the birth site of modern Spiritualism. There are words chiseled on it that have the ring of a trumpet blast:

THERE IS NO DEATH! THERE ARE NO DEAD!

Chapter 8

Missionary Martyrs

The story begins in a land of mighty hills, of vineyards and of long, blue lakes—where Ontario, Yates and Steuben Counties rub elbows. It is the story of three young people who were born and raised in that countryside many years ago.

The hero of the tale is a muscular, quiet-spoken, determined young doctor who wanted to become a minister and who became the most famous medical missionary in the history of the American West. His name was Marcus Whitman.

The other man is not exactly the villain of the piece but he is no hero. Henry Harmon Spalding was a lean, dark-haired youth whose burning eyes told of an inner hurt. He became a minister and an able one.

The heroine is a comely, vivacious girl with golden hair and a golden voice, the belle of Prattsburg in her radiant youth. Narcissa Prentiss was her name.

Both men were at various times suitors for her hand. She chose the doctor. The lives of the three young people were destined to be woven together in a strange, sad story that is part of the saga of America.

For the doctor and the blond girl the story ended in massacre and martyrdom, far from the peaceful hills of home, in a land of snow-capped mountains, majestic rivers and vengeful Indians, in a place called Oregon. The names of Marcus Whitman and Narcissa, his wife, went into the history books. The third character was denied such fame but he lived into old age and died as he had lived, ministering to the Indians in the Far West.

In Marcus Whitman's veins ran the blood of New Englanders who came to the Western New York frontier in the first year of the 19th Century. He was born in a log cabin at Rushville, then called Federal Hollow, on Sept. 4, 1802, the third son of Beza and Alice Whitman.

His father ran a tannery on the West River and by night plied the shoemaker's trade in a shop across the road from his home. Alice Whitman, a restless woman of great energy, was wont, after the children were asleep, to go and sit with her husband while he worked in his shop. One such night she left baby Marcus in his cradle near the fireplace and was startled on her return to find that a log had fallen from the fire and burned the lower part of the cradle. The infant was nearly suffocated from smoke. But for the mother's timely return, Oregon and Washington State today might be British possessions.

When Marcus was eight years old, his father died at the age of 37. Beza Whitman is buried in the little cemetery at Baldwin's Corners, one mile northeast of Rushville.

His widow remarried the year after his death and Marcus was sent to live with relatives of his father in Massachusetts. He had lived eight years on the frontier and picked up considerable forest lore that was to stand him in good stead in later years.

In New England he went to a school in Plainfield operated by a Congregationalist pastor. Among his fellow students were two young men destined for fame, William Cullen

Bryant, as a man of letters, and John Brown, as a fanatical abolitionist martyr.

Whitman longed to become a minister but lacked the funds for an education in that field. So back he came to Rushville in 1820 to begin "riding" with the village doctor. That sort of medical training was the custom of the time.

On his return to Rushville, the village that lies in two counties, Ontario and Yates, he joined the Congregational Church and began teaching a boys' Sunday-School class in the brick meeting house that still stands, well back from the principal street after 140 years. In its yard is a boulder that honors the memory of Dr. Marcus Whitman, patriot, martyr, native son and its most famous communicant.

In 1826 Marcus enrolled in the Fairfield Medical College in Herkimer County and after a 16-week course received a license to practice medicine. He practiced a few weeks at Sugartown, Pa. and for nearly three years at what is now St. Anns, Ontario, Canada, 25 miles west of Niagara Falls.

He went back to Fairfield in 1831 for another term and obtained his medical degree. At the age of 29, he returned to his native countryside and hung out his shingle at Wheeler, a hamlet along the valley road between Prattsburg and Bath. For three years he made his rounds on horseback with his saddle bags, up and down the rough roads.

When he settled in Wheeler, a struggling Presbyterian flock was building a new house of worship. The young doctor became active in the church and was made an elder and a trustee. He also interested himself in the temperance movement. The muscular young medico was an exemplary citizen, sober, industrious, clean-living, yet no prude.

There's a boulder at the crossroads in Wheeler that marks the site of his office. That weather-beaten building, now remodeled into a garage, years ago was moved back of the village postoffice. Down the road another marker points out the site of the birthplace of Henry Harmon Spalding, two years Whitman's junior, who was to cross the doctor's path so often, like a dark shadow.

In 1835 came a turning point in the career of Marcus Whitman. A Congregationalist minister, the Rev. Samuel Parker, who had served among the Indians in the St. Louis region, was touring Western New York, seeking funds and volunteers for missionary work among the tribes. He represented the missionary board of Presbyterian and Congregational churches.

He spoke in Wheeler and his story of the Indians beyond the Rockies who were eager for the white man's Book stirred the earnest young physician who had wanted to become a minister. He resolved to go West as a medical missionary, and he was a determined man.

Wheeler is only seven miles from Prattsburg and Dr. Whitman made friends in the latter village where lived Stephen Prentiss, early settler, business man and judge. Along the stream that powered his mills, Squire Prentiss lived in a sturdy one and one-half story frame house. There on March 14, 1808 was born a daughter upon whom was bestowed the unusual name of Narcissa.

The old house is still there and on its lawn is a sign telling the passerby it is the birthplace of one of America's frontier heroines. The house belongs to the Missionary Board of the Presbyterian Church and is a home for retired missionaries.

Narcissa grew up into a lissome, attractive girl with a clear, strong soprano voice which was raised in the church choir and at village get-togethers. She was one of a large family and the Prentiss home was often filled with young visitors. Then, as now, the social life of the village revolved largely around the churches.

According to some accounts, Narcissa for a time attended the Emma Willard School at Troy, one of the first girls' schools in the nation. It is certain that in 1828 she was a student at Prattsburg's Franklin Academy.

A classmate there was Henry Spalding. He proposed marriage to her and was rejected. Possibly the old judge frowned on the suit. There was a stain on Spalding's name. He had been born out of wedlock. More likely Narcissa did not love him. Whatever the reason Henry Spalding never forgot and in later years in a far place his enmity for the girl who had spurned him was revealed again and again.

On the lawn of Franklin Academy, which clings to its original name, although a modern building stands on the site of the pioneer school, are memorials to the boy and girl who were classmates there so long ago, to Narcissa Prentiss and Henry Harmon Spalding. And in the archives of the old Academy is the document by which Spalding promised to enter the Christian ministry in exchange for his tuition.

In 1833 the Prentiss family moved to Amity, now Belmont, in Allegany County. Narcissa taught in district schools in the region. In 1835 the same Samuel Parker who had fired Marcus Whitman with the desire for missionary service in the West, spoke in Angelica, a few miles from Amity. Narcissa was in the audience.

She was a devout girl. She yearned to become a worker in the mission field. She had Parker write a letter to the Mission Board asking if "females were wanted." The reply was that unmarried females weren't.

Young Doctor Whitman, who had found out that unmarried males were not too acceptable either, was told by Parker of Narcissa's ambition to become a missionary. He had met the judge's daughter in Prattsburg but they were only casual acquaintances. A whirlwind courtship ensued and when later that year Whitman left with Parker for the West, he and Narcissa were betrothed.

Whitman and Parker accompanied a fur company caravan from St. Louis to the Green River, a branch of the Colorado. They made the trip on horseback and spent much time with the Indians in what is now Wyoming and the Dakotas. Whitman, now a full-fledged medical missionary, much impressed by what he had seen, returned East to organize a missionary party for service beyond the Rockies in a strange new country beset by boundary disputes and Indians and known as Oregon.

The resolute young doctor brought back to Western New York with him two Indian boys of the Nez Perce tribe. But despite his earnest appeals, he had difficulty getting recruits for his expedition.

One day he met along the road near Howard in Steuben County an acquaintance, Henry Spalding, now an ordained minister and a graduate of Western Reserve College. With Spalding was his bride, Eliza, a plain, quiet woman from the Mohawk Valley. With Spalding also was a light wagon that made Whitman's eyes sparkle, for he had in mind just such a vehicle—to follow a trail no wagon had ever known before.

He persuaded the Spaldings to join the party, with the full knowledge that the minister had been a rejected suitor of the girl the young doctor was soon to marry. Whitman had no idea that Spalding bore a grudge. He regarded the youthful attachment as a closed incident.

A few days after the chance meeting with the Spaldings, Marcus Whitman and Narcissa Prentiss were married in the Presbyterian Church at Angelica, the shire town of Allegany County to which Judge Prentiss had recently moved.

He was 33 and she was 27. Despite her good looks and charm, Narcissa was at the age when people were beginning to call her "an old maid." They were a fine-looking couple, the sturdy, dark-eyed, dark-haired doctor and the blond girl in her severe hair-do and black bombazine dress.

At the conclusion of the ceremony the guests rose to sing in farewell Narcissa's favorite hymn, "My Native Land I Love Thee." Thinking of the perilous journey ahead of the young couple, the singers were overcome by emotion and their voices broke. But the clear, strong soprano of Narcissa carried on the song to the end.

Theirs was a hasty marriage, dictated somewhat by expediency, but as long as they lived, there was no question of the devoted love between the young couple who in February of 1835 left on a strange honeymoon trip across the continent.

And strangest of all, accompanying them was the man who a few years before had been an unsuccessful suitor for the bride's hand, the lean man with the burning eyes and the hurt in his heart, himself a recent bridegroom, the man of whom Narcissa Whitman was later to write of, with doubt and disdain, as "that man who came with us."

In 1835, when the boundaries of the United States extended only to the Rocky Mountains, a journey overland to the Pacific Coast was fraught with danger. West of St. Louis stretched barren plains, the formidable mountains, the blazing desert, a few forts and many buffalos, coyotes and none too friendly Indians.

On the Northwest coast the fur companies had established some trading posts and forts, in the little known region then called Oregon whose northern boundaries were in dispute between the United States and Britain. There was an understanding that the land would eventually go to the country that settled it first.

Before 1835 only a few hardy explorers, traders and trappers had followed the overland trail blazed by Lewis and

Clark in the early years of the century. Most travelers to the Far West—and there were not many of them—went by the long water route around the Horn. No wagon, only pack horses, had traversed the overland trail beyond the Rendezvous, the site chosen for the annual roundup of fur traders and trappers. And before Narcissa Whitman and Eliza Spalding, no white women had ever traveled the Oregon Trail.

In March of 1835 the historic journey began from Western New York, first by sleigh to Holidaysburg, Pa., thence by cable canal to Pittsburgh, and the rest of the way to St. Louis by river boat. At St. Louis the overland trail began.

At the site of Omaha the party joined a fur company caravan bound for the Rendezvous, along the Green River in what is now Southwestern Wyoming. In the Whitman party were five missionaries, three Nez Perces and two hired men. The caravan assured them protection against Indians but not against a monotonous diet of dried buffalo meat, a dish alien to New York State palates.

In a letter home Narcissa commented: "I can scarcely eat it, it appears so filthy, but it will keep us alive and we ought to be thankful for it. . . . Girls, do not waste the bread, if you knew how well I should relish it, even the driest morsel, you would save every piece carefully."

At the Rendezvous the two white women, especially the bright-haired Narcissa, attracted much attention among the motley company of rough mountain trappers, fur traders and curious Indians. Narcissa wrote that "they come and stand around our tent, peep in and grin at such strange looking objects."

After the missionaries parted with the caravan, two fur traders accompanied them across the Idaho desert where only sage brush grew. They began to encounter real hardship. Food was scarce. The horses tired. Baggage had to be cut down. The light wagon was converted into a two-wheeled cart and that had to be abandoned at the Snake River. Whitman hated to discard it. For it was a symbol.

Finally the weary travelers reached their goal—the Columbia River country with its majestic mountains, rushing rivers and lush green valleys, a veritable land of promise.

They had made history. In a little more than four months they had journeyed 2,250 miles. Narcissa and Eliza had been the first white women to cross the Rockies. The light wagon had gone farther West over the trail than any wagon had gone before. It was the vanguard of many wagons, of a mighty tide of emigration which eventually determined that Oregon Territory should be a part of the United States and not of Great Britain.

The Whitmans went West to save souls. They also helped save a commonwealth for their native land.

In Oregon Spalding picked his mission site among the friendly Nez Perce Indians. Whitman had to accept a place near Fort Walla Walla among the Cayuses, a troublesome, suspicious tribe. It was at Waiilatpu, which meant in the Indian language, "the place of the rye grass."

The doctor built the adobe dwelling that was to be his and Narcissa's home for 11 years, the first real American home West of the Rockies. He plowed the land and set out an orchard. He built a saw mill and in three years had established a mission, a school and a farm, and he and his wife learned the Indian language. The clear soprano voice of the young woman that had dominated village choirs in Western New York charmed the savages, especially the children, in this wild new land.

The doctor ministered to the physical ills of the Indians, as well as to their spiritual needs. The Cayuses were a superstitious, vengeful lot. They killed their own medicine men

106

when the native voodoo magic failed. Continually the threat of death hung over Marcus Whitman. But he was ever patient with the Indians, even when they threatened him.

The young couple knew many sorrows. A baby girl was born to them, with blue eyes and fair hair. She was the joy of Narcissa's heart. One day when the child was only two years old, she toddled off, unseen, to the river and was drowned.

There was friction and jealousy within the church. Spalding seemed bent on causing trouble for the girl who had jilted him in Prattsburg years before. He undermined the Whitmans with the national mission board and in 1842 the doctor was ordered to take a transfer. Whitman was thoroughly aroused. He did not want to move. He sensed the strategic location of his mission on the Oregon Trail and he visualized a wave of migration to the frontier. He determined to fight the board's edict—right in the board's home office in Boston.

So in the late Fall of 1842 Marcus Whitman set out for the East on horseback with a male companion, back over the perilous trail he knew so well, in bitter weather, on a ride that was to make history.

In the East he was a strange figure, bearded and clad in mountain garb, buckskin breeches, long buffalo overcoat and hood. He attracted attention wherever he went. And that did not harm his cause.

He appeared before the mission board and finally won his point. There would be no transfer. In New York he visited Horace Greeley and made a good impression on the editor. He also went to Washington and about that visit a legend grew.

Whitman's admirers have claimed that he virtually single-handed saved Oregon for the Union; that he dissuaded President Tyler and Secretary of State Webster from trading

Oregon to the British for a codfishery off Newfoundland. Later-day historians have exploded that story.

But the doctor did see important officials in Washington, among them John C. Spencer of Canandaigua, then secretary of the treasury. And he presented the case for Oregon well. He gave first hand information on the richness of the country. He proved that wagons could go over the long trail. His crowning achievement was, on his return West in 1843, in leading an emigrant train of 200 wagons to Oregon over that trail.

So in a sense Marcus Whitman may have saved Oregon. The emigration of 1843, forerunner of a rush of settlers to the West, was a determining factor in the territory's eventual annexation to the Union.

Back in Oregon Whitman found that Indians had burned his mill during his absence. A Cayuse had invaded the privacy of his home and Narcissa had to seek refuge in the nearby fort. She had been ill and in her heart was the constant ache for the child who had drowned.

The emigrant wagons kept rolling in and the Whitman house was always crowded. Narcissa mothered orphaned youngsters and the heartache eased a little.

There was a reconciliation with the Spaldings but trouble loomed on other fronts. Whitman viewed with misgivings the establishment of a Catholic mission nearby. He feared its effect on the Indians who would discern a lack of religious unity among the whites.

In 1847 an epidemic broke out among the Cayuses. The doctor did his best—and he was an able physician—but many tribesmen died. The superstitious Indians blamed the paleface doctor whose magic did not work. Whitman's life was in danger and he knew it. But he would stick it out and he uttered these prophetic words:

"My death will probably do as much good for Oregon as my life can."

It was the noon hour of a cold and foggy November 29 in 1847 that the Indians came. The doctor was reading before the fire and the house was full of emigrants and their children. A tomahawk struck Whitman down but he did not die at once. Narcissa was shot and she staggered downstairs to pillow her golden head on her husband's breast. They died together, in a scene of bloody horror, far from the peaceful Upstate hills they had left 11 years before on their honeymoon.

There were 20 persons in and around the mission house that day of massacre. Fourteen either were killed or died of their wounds. Eleven of them were men and two were children. Narcissa was the only woman slain. Six escaped. Henry Spalding had spent the night in the Whitman house and was down the trail only a few miles when the Indians struck. He missed death by only a few hours.

The massacre aroused a storm of wrath in Oregon. Troops and posses mobilized and the Cayuses fled to the hills. Finally they surrendered five of the tribe as ringleaders in the slaughter and the five were hanged.

In the nation's capital the story of the Whitman's martyrdom stirred the lawmakers to action and in 1848, a few months after the massacre, President Polk signed a bill making Oregon a territory of the United States. Out of that territory came two great states, Oregon and Washington.

Marcus and Narcissa had not died in vain.

Henry Spalding spent the rest of his days as a missionary to the Western Indians and died in Idaho at the age of 72.

The Whitmans are not forgotten in the West they helped to win. At Walla Walla, Wash. is Whitman College of the

Congregational Church and on its campus is Narcissa Prentiss Hall.

There's a tall monument on the hill near their graves at "the place of the rye grass." And a Whitman National Forest in the Blue Mountains and a Whitman County in the State of Washington.

When in the 1880s the Tacoma, Wash. chapter of the Daughters of the American Revolution presented a public drinking fountain to the city in commemoration of the martyred Narcissa, prominent in the dedicatory parade was a band made up of young Indians, descendants of those who took part in the massacre.

Atop the Witherspoon Building which houses the national Presbyterian headquarters in Philadelphia, Marcus Whitman stands in sculptured stone in his frontier garb, a wagon wheel beside him.

Nor are the martyrs forgotten in the land of their nativity. Today the modern highway from Penn Yan to Rushville that was a rough country road when a young doctor made his calls on horseback is called the Marcus Whitman Highway.

And the road that winds through the vine-clad countryside from Naples to Narcissa's birthplace is the Narcissa Prentiss Highway.

In Prattsburg the community meeting place in the Presbyterian Church is called Narcissa Prentiss Hall. At church and community gatherings they still sing Narcissa's song, the one that was sung at her wedding, "My Native Land I Love Thee."

They loved their native land well, the strong young doctor and the girl with the golden hair, who live in history as heroic figures of their time.

Chapter 9

Political "Siamese Twins"

One Summer day in 1824 a coach lost a wheel, overturned and spilled its occupants into a muddy ditch in the young village of Rochester.

Among the passengers in the capsized coach was a scrawny, red-haired, eagle-beaked, cigar-smoking young lawyer from Auburn. Among the local citizens who came to the rescue and helped get the coach going again was a burly, lantern-jawed, swarthy, affable young editor.

Writing of the incident in after years, the lawyer recalled that "among the crowd was one taller and more effective, more deferential and sympathizing than the rest, who lent the party his assistance."

The tall editor was Thurlow Weed. The runty lawyer was William Henry Seward. It was their first meeting and out of it grew a life-long friendship and a political alliance that made history.

For some 30 years the pair controlled the machinery of, first the Whig party, then the Republicans, in New York State. Their influence was felt in national circles and they had a hand in making Presidents and Presidential candidates.

Weed was the manager of the team, the strategist and party boss who manipulated men and measures behind the scenes.

Seward was "the front man," who went out and coralled the votes and made the speeches.

Weed craved power. Seward craved office. The ambitions of both were gratified in generous measure. But the grand prize eluded the partners. Thurlow Weed was able to make his crony Governor and United States Senator but he failed to put Bill Seward in the White House.

At the time of their fateful first meeting in Rochester in 1824, the two ambitious young men were only on the first steps of their climb to the heights. Their backgrounds were as dissimilar as their personalities.

Poverty and struggle marked Thurlow Weed's early years. He was born in 1797 in Greene County, New York. His family was wretchedly poor and his father was a failure, who even spent some time in jail for debt.

When Thurlow was two years old, the family moved to Catskill and the boy grew up in that romantic Hudson River countryside. He had only a few months of schooling. At the age of eight he was blowing the bellows in a blacksmith shop. He worked as a handy man in a tavern, and as a cabin boy on a Hudson River boat. He enjoyed mixing with people. During his spare time he hung around the office of the *Catskill Recorder* and when he was 11 he was given work as an odd job man in the print shop. His love for the Fourth Estate and for the smell of printer's ink never left him.

But soon the Weeds were moving their humble belongings again, this time to Cincinnatus in Cortland County. On that frontier life was more primitive than in the long-settled Hudson River town. Thurlow worked on farms, finally got a job as an apprentice printer. In 1812 the war drums rolled and young Weed joined the militia. At the age of 15 he was shouldering a musket on occasional patrol duty along Lake Ontario. He never saw combat, but he was appointed quartermaster sergeant of his regiment, indicating the stripling had recognized executive ability.

He worked at the printer's trade in several Upstate towns after the war. One of them was Cooperstown and it was there he fell in love with the daughter of his landlady. Catherine Ostrander reciprocated his affection but her mother looked askance at this wandering young printer, and it was three years before they were married. That was in 1818.

In the meantime Weed had worked in New York and Albany, where he got his first experience in lobbying—as a representative of the Typographical Union which was seeking the right to incorporate. At the same time he began writing editorials. At first his style was clumsy and his grammar faulty. But he studied hard and it was not long before he had overcome his early deficiencies.

After his marriage Weed bought his first paper, a small weekly in Norwich, the *Republican Agriculturalist* (The editor could not even spell the name of his own paper correctly then). Weed supported DeWitt Clinton and the Erie Canal project. In less than two years mounting debts forced him to fold the paper. He tried publishing a weekly in Manlius and again went broke.

One September day in 1821, Everard Peck, owner of the *Telegraph* in the budding young town of Rochester, looked up to see a tall, swarthy, hazel-eyed young man at his desk. The young man said he wanted a job. At first Peck said "No opening." As the stranger turned away, Peck noticed quick tears come to his eyes. The kind-hearted publisher called his visitor back. He hired Thurlow Weed as a printer and junior editor at $400 a year and advanced him money for rent and groceries.

It was the turning point in Weed's hitherto feckless career. In Rochester he plunged into politics and soon was trading brickbats with the rival papers. Weed followed the banners of John Quincy Adams and DeWitt Clinton. In 1824 his stock rose in the village on the Genesee when he went to Albany to lobby for a charter for a new bank in Rochester and won his case over the strong opposition of Canandaigua. At the same time he made valuable contacts in Albany.

Weed was a coming man in the raw young mill town of some 4,000 population in 1824 when he and Seward met for the first time.

The beginnings of William Henry Seward were by no means as humble as those of his partner in politics. He was born in the village of Florida, Orange County, in 1801. He was of mixed Welsh, English and Irish descent.

His father, Dr. Samuel S. Seward, was a physician, businessman, political boss, onetime judge, a Columbia College graduate, a Democrat and a slaveholder. From his boyhood, when he saw slaves serving in his own home, William Seward abhorred human bondage.

The delicate, undersized, fair complected, red-headed boy attended Goshen Academy and excelled in debate. At the age of 15 he entered Union College at Schenectady—as a sophomore.

In later years he was careless about his dress but in college his ill-fitting homespun garb humiliated him. He ordered new clothes and when his father, a difficult man always, refused to pay the tailor's bill, young Seward left college in the middle of his senior year, without a word to his parents or to the venerated President of Union, Dr. Eliphalet Nott.

The 18-year old student turned up in Georgia as principal of an academy. There he saw the slave system at close hand and it influenced his thinking in after years. He yielded to his mother's pleas and came home, to resume his studies at Union with the beginning of the new term. He was graduated in 1820 at the age of 19. In college his chief distinction was as a speaker. He detested mathematics but was a creditable scholar in Latin and Greek.

After his graduation, he read law in a New York City office for 18 months. In the metropolis he heard much talk of politics and became interested in public affairs.

On being admitted to the bar in 1823, young Seward decided to settle in the new Western section of the state and it was not long before his shingle was swinging in the breeze in the thriving village of Auburn on Owasco Lake.

Auburn then was the chief town West of Albany, with a population of 2,000, a new state prison, a new divinity school, abundant water power and a place on the main trail between Albany and Niagara, a road choked with Westward-bound emigrant wagons.

Another inducement drew Seward to the Finger Lakes village. It was an affair of the heart. Auburn was the home of Frances Miller, a classmate of Seward's sister at the Emma Willard School in Troy. The two young people had met and liked each other.

It chanced that Frances' father, Elijah Miller, a former county judge, political power and leading citizen of Auburn, was getting old and needed a bright young lawyer in his office. Frances' boy friend, the ambitious, ingratiating, well-educated Bill Seward, was just the man the judge wanted. Soon the young man was carrying much of the court room and desk work as a member of the law firm of Miller & Seward.

The little redhead stepped easily into the life of the village. He loved the town and the surrounding countryside with its lakes, hills, waterfalls, glens and caverns. He was to travel far but always he came home happily to Auburn. To him it was ever "Sweet Auburn, loveliest village of the plain."

Seward took a keen interest in community affairs. He joined the militia, headed a debating society, attended political meetings at which he often served as secretary. He discarded his inherited Federalism and became an ardent supporter of Clinton, the Erie Canal and all internal improvements. His switch may have been influenced by the fact that his prospective father-in-law, Judge Miller, was a Clintonian.

In 1824 the young lawyer delivered the Fourth of July oration at the Auburn celebration. He was a rising star in politics and in the law, betrothed to the daughter of the local bigwig. His future was roseate. And then he met Thurlow Weed, who was to be his alter ego for 40 years.

* * *

After their chance meeting in Rochester, Seward looked up Weed whenever his law business took him to Rochester. Their acquaintance ripened into a warm friendship. In a few years the two families were exchanging visits.

It was the Morgan affair, one of the strangest chapters in American history, that first bound them together in politics. William Morgan, an obscure and disgruntled bricklayer, had threatened to publish the secrets of Free Masonry and in 1826 he had been kidnaped from Canandaigua jail and driven in a closed carriage to Fort Niagara. He was never seen alive again and ugly stories were circulated that he had been done to death by Free Masons to silence him.

Mass meetings were held and Western New York became the center of a turmoil that split families and broke old political ties. The wrath against the secret order was fiercest among the farmers and workman, for most of the upper crust were Masons. When prosecution of members of the order accused in the kidnaping was delayed and key witnesses disappeared, the tension mounted and Anti Masonry became a political issue. Free Masons were dropped from local tickets, lodges went into hiding or disbanded and a new national organization, the Anti Masonic party, eventually evolved.

In Rochester, Weed now, part owner of the *Telegraph,* watched the gathering storm with shrewd eyes. He had served a term in the State Assembly and in winning that office, had learned much about rough and tumble politics. He had refused to print Morgan's expose of Masonry. Later he turned down the chance to print Joseph Smith's Mormon bible.

Weed jumped into the Anti Masonic fray with both fists. He went with the local citizens investigating committee to Niagara and, convinced that there had been foul play, he campaigned in his newspaper for a thorough investigation. His organ became a leading spokesman of the movement.

When in 1827 a body was washed up along Lake Ontario, he instigated an inquest that declared that the dead man was the missing Morgan. A later inquest found that the body was that of a Canadian named Munroe. At that time a cynical remark was attributed to Weed that was to haunt him for years. Although he denied it, his enemies claimed he said the body "was a good enough Morgan until after the election."

Weed established a newspaper, the *Anti Masonic Enquirer,* in Rochester to further the cause of the party, which was spreading far beyond Western New York. In 1830, a recognized leader of the movement, he left Rochester to take the helm of an Albany Anti Masonic sheet, the *Evening Journal,* a newspaper he was to make one of the most powerful political organs in the nation.

Other young, ambitious men had become identified with the new party. Among them were the aristocratic Francis

Granger of Canandaigua; a bland, self-educated lawyer from Buffalo, Millard Fillmore, and William H. Seward of Auburn.

Seward had been increasingly active in local politics. In 1827 he had been nominated for surrogate of Cayuga County but a hostile Senate had rejected the appointment. He was a vigorous supporter of John Quincy Adams in the losing campaign of 1828. The next year he joined the Anti Masons and was a delegate to the state convention of that party in 1829. In 1830 he was a delegate to the national convention which nominated William Wirt for President. The young Auburn eagle was spreading his wings.

In 1830, at the urging of his friend Weed, he ran for the State Senate on the Anti Masonic ticket and won by a slim margin. In Albany he worked closely with Weed, who was carefully building a state machine. Seward, although one of the youngest Senators, was regarded as the ablest of the Anti Masonic minority.

Weed drew up the strategy of the party and Seward drafted the statements and speeches. He also fought for internal improvements and worked for a lateral canal which would serve his home town, bypassed by the Clinton Ditch.

Seward was re-elected to the Senate in 1832. By 1834 Weed and his allies saw that the Anti Masonic party had no future. It had served its purpose of dividing the opposition and it had been used by Weed as a springboard to power. Weed, now in the boss's saddle, tossed it aside as he would discard a dead cigar and led his allies, Seward, Granger and the rest, into the new Whig party, an amalgam of many forces, with the common aim of routing the Jackson-Van Buren Democracy.

By that time the fortunes of Thurlow Weed, the boss, and William Seward, the statesman, were inextricably bound together. Seward was to say in after years: "Weed is Seward and Seward is Weed and each approves what the other says and does." That was an exaggeration, for the pair frequently differed, but for 40 years the two men, bound together by a genuine affection as well as by political ambition, were as David and Jonathan.

The partners complemented each other. Seward, sometimes erratic and impulsive, leaned on the sober common sense of the older man. Weed admired Seward's brilliance, his flair for words, his erudition. They made an effective team.

Weed, who began life as a country bumpkin, acquired a cultivated air and wore fine broadcloth. Seward, college bred and a sophisticate, affected wrinkled garb and a countrified, bantering manner.

A political foe, William L. Marcy, dubbed Weed "The Jolly Drummer." He shone in the caucus, the committee room, the lobby. He had a persuasive, confidential manner and he made every man with whom he talked feel he was his special friend.

To gain his ends, he cajoled, threatened, stormed, made deals—whatever the situation demanded. He never was over-scrupulous in his political methods, but like most bosses, he kept his word once it was given. He was a shrewd judge of men. He knew every remote district in the state and every crossroads politician. Like two other masters of practical politics, James G. Blaine and James A. Farley, he never forgot a name or a face. Nor did he ever forget an act of treachery or double dealing.

The ruddy-faced six-footer was the soul of geniality as he presided over the wine and the oysters but his enemies found he could be savage and vituperative in politics. In an era of "personal journalism" he called names with the best of them and he was involved in many libel suits, both as plaintiff and defendant.

Basically a conservative, he was always realistic and believed the end justified the means. As his political power grew, so did his craving for money. No doubt memories of his poverty-stricken boyhood spurred his chase for dollars. At any rate he amassed a fortune and about it clung an aura of corruption. He openly lobbied for railroad and traction interests and was closely allied with many lords of business and industry.

Seward was a more complex character and full of contradictions. He had a broad streak of idealism in his makeup but expediency was his god. John Quincy Adams was his youthful idol and he strove to emulate the career of the "Old Man Eloquent." But he lacked Adams' moral stamina and the high-minded statesman too often gave way to the blind partisan, his lofty idealism forgotten in his itch for office. Before Seward's eyes the portals of a white mansion on the Potomac beckoned—even in his dreams.

The fidgety little man with the puckered face, the shaggy brows and the eternal cigar inherited some of the mysticism of his Welsh forebears. He had imagination and a broad philosophical outlook. He showed courage—sometimes. He had a taste for intrigue. He was a subtle, adroit opportunist, always able to bound back from his mistakes.

Many of the elders of his party distrusted him. They considered him erratic and unstable. He talked too much and at the wrong times and his rashness often worried Weed.

Seward was on good terms with his political foes, even the Southern firebrands, when he was the spokesman in Congress for the anti-slavery forces.

When Jefferson Davis was secretary of war in the Pierce cabinet, Senator Seward was a frequent visitor at the Davis

The Fox Sisters, Margaret, Katie and Leah. Fowler's
Monstrous Octagon House.

Thurlow Weed, William H. Seward, Millard Fillmore.

home. When Mrs. Davis was critically ill in child birth and a great blizzard raged in Washington, Seward ordered his sleigh and carriage horses to take the woman who was nursing Mrs. Davis to the Secretary's home. Even in the bitterness of the war, the Davises remembered Seward's kindness.

His private life, like that of his partner Weed, was impeccable. He was an affectionate husband and father. He was well liked by his Auburn neighbors. He was kind to the downtrodden, especially Negroes. He was beloved by his intimates because of his generous, outgiving nature. He liked cards and small supper parties.

His effectiveness as a speaker was marred by his husky voice, the result of a chronic catarrhal condition. He spoke in a conversational tone, pacing the floor as he talked, as if addressing a jury. He would take a pinch of snuff and sneeze into a yellow handkerchief. He would twirl his eyeglasses as he leaned against a pillar. Always he spoke with confidence. And as he frankly admitted, he hardly ever spoke from conviction.

The elements were mixed in William Henry Seward.

In 1834, upon the dissolution of the Anti Masons in New York State, Weed began building up Seward and won for his friend the Whig nomination for Governor. Seward lost by 10,000 votes to the Democrat, Marcy, and went back to the serenity of his Auburn home and his growing law practice.

He became associated with a group of speculators who had taken over the Holland Company's lands in Chautauqua County and spent two years in that county, adjusting matters. It was a task requiring all his tact and diplomatic skill, because angry farmers had stormed the land office at Mayville. Seward smoothed matters over, but lost money eventually in his land investment.

The panic of 1837 brightened Whig chances and Weed began grooming Seward for the gubernatorial race of 1838. Although Francis Granger craved the honor, Weed put Seward over in the convention, managed his campaign and saw his crony elected by 10,000 votes. That victory ended the long rule of the old Albany Regency of Van Buren and Marcy in the state. And Thurlow Weed got the state printing, a juicy plum.

Seward was re-elected Governor in 1840, but by a reduced majority. He was swept into office on the wings of the Harrison-Tyler landslide. General Winfield Scott had been Weed's first choice for the Whig Presidential nomination, but he had jumped on the bandwagon of another war hero, William Henry Harrison.

As Governor, Seward pursued a liberal course, which made him unpopular with the conservative Whig leaders. He put through a spending program for expansion of the canals and the new railroads. He fought for admission of immigrant children into the New York City public schools. He befriended the Indians. He settled, temporarily, at least, anti-rent troubles in the Hudson Valley where farmers were in revolt against the archaic patroon system.

Although never an abolitionist, Seward consistently opposed the extension of slavery and as Governor pushed through a law granting trial by jury to fugitive slaves caught in New York. He feuded with the Governor of Virginia, who demanded the return to that state of three Negro sailors accused of helping slaves escape.

At the end of his second term he announced he would not be a candidate for re-election. The chances are he would not have won again. His liberal school policy had made him enemies and in later years when Nativism flowered like the Ku Klux Klan of our time, his record arose to haunt him.

Seward liked to tell two anecdotes of his gubernatorial

years. Once, while traveling on a stage coach, he mentioned to the driver that he was the Governor. The driver looked over the runty man in the wrinkled clothes and said he did not believe him. "All right," said Seward, "ask the next innkeeper." That innkeeper was a friend of Seward, but he had to have his joke. When Seward asked him, "Am I not the Governor of the state?," the tavern man answered: "You are not." "Well, then who is?," persisted Seward. "Thurlow Weed!" came the swift answer.

On another occasion when the Governor journeyed to the Eastern part of the state to look into the anti-rent dispute, he was accompanied by Judge Sackett of Seneca Falls, a tall, portly, well-groomed gentleman who carried a gold-headed cane. The crowds that turned out to greet the Governor gave their cheers to the imposing Judge. They did not figure the bird-like little man could be the state's chief executive. One observer once likened Seward to a "wise Macaw."

Seward went back to Auburn, nailed up his old tin sign again and worked hard at the law to recoup his losses in land speculation. He specialized in patent law, traveled widely and tried cases before the United States Supreme Court. He lived in the late judge's mansion now, with his wife and their two sons, Frederick and Augustus, and he planted trees and bushes on the grounds and basked in the serenity of "the loveliest village."

In 1846 he performed the most unselfish and humane act of his career. At the risk of bodily harm to himself and at cost to his prestige and popularity, he defended without fee a young Negro murderer, William Freeman, in his home town of Auburn.

Seward believed that the youth who had senselessly slain four persons should be confined as a lunatic and not be executed for his crime. He defied public clamor for vengeance and during the two Freeman trials was jeered and jostled by crowds on the streets of Auburn. He lost his case and had an appeal pending when the young Negro died in his cell.

William H. Seward made many notable speeches during his long career but none of them came so straight from the heart as these words he spoke in defense of William Freeman:

"This prisoner is a convict, a pauper, a Negro, without intellect, sense or emotion. I am not the prisoner's lawyer. I am indeed a volunteer in his behalf but society and mankind have the deepest interests. I am the lawyer for society and mankind, shocked beyond expression at the scene I have witnessed here—of trying a maniac as a malefactor. There is not a white man or a white woman who would not have been dismissed long since from the peril of such a prosecution."

During the five years (1843-1848) that Seward was out of office, Weed's political fortunes were in eclipse. He had lost control of his party in the state and the Democrats were in the saddle in Washington. The boss took a European trip and washed his hands of the Clay-Polk campaign. He was no admirer of Henry Clay nor was Seward. But Horace Greeley, the New York editor, who had been admitted to a limited junior partnership in the political firm of Weed & Seward, was. In those days Greeley was kept in check by the other partners. They humored his whims because they needed his powerful pen. But Weed denied the moonfaced journalist the offices he craved.

When 1848 rolled around, things were looking up for the Whig legions. The New York Democracy was split over the slavery extension issue into two blocs, the Barnburners or free soilers, and the conservative Hunkers. Weed scented victory in the air and went to work. "The Jolly Drummer" was one of the first to beat the drums for General Zachary Taylor, the Mexican War hero, and had much to do with getting the Whig presidential nomination for "Old Rough and Ready" over Clay. He had his hands full keeping Taylor from writing impolitic—and ungrammatical—letters.

At Weed's behest, Seward returned to the political wars and took the stump for Taylor. He did not relish the presence on the ticket of Millard Fillmore, once an ally, now a bitter rival. Fillmore got the Vice Presidential nomination as a sop to his disgruntled leader, Clay. In the Fall of 1848 Taylor and Fillmore won a resounding victory and the Whigs captured the state legislature. That opened the way for Weed to achieve another goal—send his friend Seward to the United States Senate. He had his way and in March of 1849 Senator Seward went to Washington.

He found the Senate a battleground over the extension of slavery into new states, a problem that arose with the gaining of new territory after the War with Mexico. Clay came forward with his famous Compromise, which would admit California as a free state, establish territorial governments in the other lands ceded by Mexico and provide more rigid enforcement of the fugitive slave law.

In the stormy debate over the proposals, Seward, although a freshman senator, became the leader of the anti-slavery forces. In one of his speeches he declared that "there is a higher Law than the Constitution." The phrase was widely quoted and was interpreted to mean that the laws of humanity should transcend man-made documents. What Seward intended was never entirely clear.

On taking office, President Taylor aimed to split the New York patronage between Weed, Seward & Co. and Fillmore giving the major share to the Vice President. Soon Weed and Seward edged into the good graces of the new President. Seward was a frequent visitor and advisor at the White

House and became recognized as the leader of the administration forces in the Senate. Weed and Seward gobbled most of the New York patronage and Fillmore was out in the cold.

Then Taylor died unexpectedly and Fillmore moved into the White House. Its portals were closed to Weed and Seward. Henry Clay became the administration spokesman in the Senate and the Compromise prevailed. Meanwhile the Fillmore forces declared war on the old machine in New York.

A test of strength came in the 1850 state convention which nominated, without a fight, Washington Hunt, a middle of the roader, for Governor, but split over a resolution endorsing Seward's course. When a majority supported the Senator, a group of Fillmore men, led by Frank Granger, walked out of the hall. Because of the silver mane of their leader, the bolters were known as "The Silver Grays."

Fillmore failed in his bid for a renomination and Seward had a lot to do with that. The Whig candidate of 1852, Gen. Winfield Scott, went down to overwhelming defeat and the handwriting was on the wall for the Whig party. Weed and Seward sensed it, but they held off from joining the new sectional party which called itself Republican.

For, first of all, Seward had to be re-elected to the Senate and he needed the support of the remaining Whigs. When that was accomplished, the "Siamese Twins" of politics deserted the Whig standard and joined the Republicans, just as a quarter of a century earlier they had abandoned the Anti Masonic party for the Whigs. It was not long before Senator Seward was the new party's best known leader in the nation.

He yearned for the Republican Presidential nomination in 1856 but Weed held him back. Seward's liberal school policy toward immigrants was remembered with bitterness by the Nativists, then at their peak. Besides the boss was waiting for 1860.

126

So the Republicans nominated John Charles Fremont and Seward took the stump for the Pathfinder who never found the path to the White House. The heavy vote the Republicans rolled up convinced Seward and Weed that theirs was the party of the future.

On Oct. 25, 1858, Seward made a speech in Rochester's Corinthian Hall that stirred the nation. In his sepulchral voice, he warned his Republican audience of "an irrepressible conflict between opposite and enduring forces . . . It means that the United States will sooner or later become either a slave-holding nation or entirely a free nation." The phrase, "irrepressible conflict" went into the history books and Seward's backers were called "the Irrepressibles."

The logical-minded Seward saw that the sectional clash was basically economic and political and although he genuinely hated human bondage, he considered the moral issue of slavery secondary. This paradoxical man who boasted he had no convictions was constant in one cause—the preservation of the Union.

The war clouds gathered, the Southern belligerency mounted and soon Seward was hedging, explaining, pleading with both sides to avoid the conflict he had declared "irrepressible."

With the Democrats hopelessly split along sectional lines, all the omens spelled a Republican victory in 1860. Weed felt the time was ripe to make his crony, Bill Seward, President of the United States.

The New York boss led a big and confident delegation, armed with bands, cigars and champagne, to the Republican convention in the Chicago's vast new wooden Wigwam. Most observers thought Seward's nomination was in the bag. He was by far the best known of the aspirants.

The Senator stayed in Auburn and his fellow townsmen

hauled a cannon onto the lawn of his mansion, ready to fire it the minute the victory flash came from Chicago.

In that gusty city on Lake Michigan, Weed was having his troubles. Leaders were looking around for a "more available" candidate than Seward. The New Yorker had been tied too closely to the anti-slavery forces. He had made too many speeches, taken too many stands, made too many enemies.

Illinois had an "available" candidate in Abraham Lincoln, a gaunt, homely, wise-cracking lawyer and former Congressman, who had few enemies and was known to the country only through his debates with Stephen A. Douglas, "the Little Giant" of the Democracy, on the slavery question.

Lincoln's managers made some deals, including the swapping of two cabinet posts for the support of the big Pennsylvania and Indiana delegations. Greeley, who had broken with Weed, Seward & Co. because he had been denied the public offices he craved, labored effectively among the delegates against his old partners.

So Lincoln carried off the prize. In the Wigwam Thurlow Weed buried his face in his hands and wept like a child. Seward's Auburn neighbors sadly hauled their cannon home, unfired.

At first Seward was inclined to sulk in his tent after his defeat but Weed prodded him into taking the stump for the Republican ticket. Striving for party harmony, the New York boss established close relations with the Lincoln camp.

After the Republican victory over a divided Democracy, Seward served his country well in the agonizing period between Lincoln's election and inauguration. While Buchanan in the White House vacillated and Lincoln kept silent at Springfield, the Senator tried to cool off the Southern secessionists. He did not understand that the Union meant one thing to the North and another to the South and believed that the Southern people eventually would be loyal to the old flag. He misjudged their sentiments. His was a futile effort but his adroit campaign of conciliation gained some time for his cause.

In the interest of party harmony Lincoln felt bound to offer the state department portfolio to the man who had been his principal rival at Chicago and who commanded so large a following. Seward accepted and resigned his seat in the Senate. When Horace Greeley had a good chance of winning the vacant place, Weed evened up old scores with the editor by tipping the scales for Ira Harris.

When he entered the cabinet, Seward figured he could dominate Lincoln. He was disillusioned when the President overruled his secretary's more fantastic plans, such as keeping the Union together by waging war on England. When Seward saw Lincoln was the boss, he changed front, followed his leader and came to admit that "Mr. Lincoln is the best of us."

It is generally conceded that after a bad start, Seward made a capable wartime secretary of state. He and Lincoln became warm friends and the President saved Seward when a cabal of Radical senators demanded the secretary's ouster. The weary President enjoyed swapping jokes with Seward, whose informal ways contrasted with the stuffy, sanctimonious manner of such men as Secretary of the Treasury Chase.

Lincoln liked the bluff Weed, too. The latter wielded considerable influence in Washington during the war. It has been charged that he used it to make commissions on war contracts. Certainly he made a barrel of money during the conflict. He also helped recruit men and supplies and went to England as an ambassador of good will to the press in a critical period. Weed's love for the Union was as sincere as his worship of Mammon.

But in his own state the old chief's grip on his party was slipping. He could not prevent the nomination for governor in 1862 of the Genesee Valley grandee, General James S. Wadsworth, a former Democrat. Seward had his hands full in Washington and did not mix in state politics.

In 1863 Weed sold his *Journal* and soon was living in New York. He supported Lincoln's re-election and gained control of the state committee of the Union party, the label the Republicans took for the campaign of '64. But he could not control the state convention which chose the wily Reuben E. Fenton of Chautauqua County for governor. Fenton won and grabbed for the driver's reins. Weed's power was waning fast.

The war ended and Lincoln was slain. Seward, too, was marked for death and was stabbed in his own home by one of the Booth gang, the brutish Payne. The secretary was in critical condition for weeks.

Seward and Weed took a moderate position toward the conquered South and were at odds with the vengeful Radicals, led by Sumner, Wade and Stevens. The New Yorkers supported Andrew Johnson in his desperate fight with the Radical bloc. Weed joined an ill-starred coalition movement of Johnson Republicans and Union Democrats. It was no use. The Radicals were in the saddle.

By 1868 Weed had completely lost control of the New York organization. Fenton and young Roscoe Conkling, handsome and arrogant, were the stars of the party show. Seward became a "has been," too. After his cabinet term expired, he made two trips around the world, in 1869-1870, and wrote of his travels.

Back in Auburn, he began writing his autobiography. He was stricken with paralysis and died on Oct. 9, 1872 in the family home. That big gray mansion where stone lions crouch at the gates and griffins guard the entrance has been preserved as a historical landmark. Until a few years ago descendants of the statesman were living there.

Seward sleeps in a shady dell in Auburn's Fort Hill Cemetery. A simple stone stands at his grave.

In his autobiography, harking back to the excitement over his defense of the Negro, Freeman, Seward wrote:

"Perhaps years hence when the passion which agitates this community shall have passed away, some wandering stranger . . . may erect over my remains a humble stone and thereon put this epitaph: 'He Was Faithful.' "

Near Seward's grave is an ornamental urn. At its base are graven these words: "He Was Faithful."

It is ironical that William Henry Seward should walk forever in history in the more massive shadow of a man he thought his inferior—that he is remembered only as "Lincoln's secretary of state."

Thurlow Weed lived for a decade after he stood weeping at Seward's bier. He outlived all his contemporaries—Fillmore, Greeley, Raymond, Seward. Out of power in his late years, he watched with keen old eyes every turn of the political wheel he had once manipulated.

The old man lived much in the past. He made pilgrimages to Cooperstown, to Rochester and other scenes of his youth. He began writing his memoirs but, like Seward, he died before they were done and other hands completed his autobiography.

Thurlow Weed passed away on the morning of Nov. 22, 1882 in his New York home. He had lived 85 eventful years. The "wizard of the lobby" sleeps on a hill above Albany, the city where he had risen to the political heights.

He left an estate of nearly a million dollars.

Chapter 10

The Forgotten President

Of all the Presidents, only Andrew Jackson and Abraham Lincoln sprang from such humble beginnings.

None of the 34 men who have lived in the White House was more handsome and distinguished in appearance.

And none is so completely forgotten as is Millard Fillmore, 13th President of the United States.

The 19th Century was seven days old when a son was born to Nathaniel and Phoebe Millard Fillmore in their log cabin in the forest frontier of Central New York. Even today the site, near Summer Hill in Cayuga County, is a remote and lonely spot in the rough hill country southeast of Moravia.

The Fillmores were so poor they had no cradle for their first born son. A wooden sap trough had to serve.

The family was of hardy English-New England stock. Millard's grandfather, John Fillmore, was a seaman who shed glory on the name by capturing a pirate captain.

When the boy was two years old, his father lost his land through a faulty title and the family moved a few miles to a town with the improbable name of Semipronius. There Nathaniel leased 130 heavily wooded, untilled acres, built a log house and began clearing the land.

So it was that from early boyhood Millard Fillmore knew

hard work on a frontier farm. He could attend the district school only two or three months in the Winter.

In 1814 when the boy, who was large for his age, talked of enlisting in the War of 1812, his father received a call from an acquaintance, one Benjamin Hungerford, who ran a carding and wool dressing mill at Sparta in the Genesee Country.

The senior Fillmore, wishing to forestall his son's going to war, asked Hungerford to take the boy home with him for four months and teach him the cloth dressing trade. As Hungerford had a heavy load for his team to haul through the woods, Millard walked most of the 100 miles. He had never been out of sight of home before.

Old settlers in Sparta in later years recalled the well built, round-faced, fair haired lad, dressed in homespun gray coat and trousers, wool hat and stout cowhide boots, as quiet, friendly, deliberate in speech and movement.

As Fillmore recalled in his reminiscences, published in his old age, Hungerford, instead of putting him to work at the mill as he had agreed, set the boy to chopping wood and other menial chores.

For a time the young man bore it in silence. But when at dusk, after a hard day in woods, his employer ordered Millard to chop some wood for the shop, the future President rebelled. He told the man he had come to learn a trade, that he already knew how to chop wood. Hungerford charged him with insolence and threatened to punish him. Thereupon Millard raised the axe menacingly and his employer walked away. After that the 14-year old boy, who had shown such an independent spirit, worked in the woolen mill and there was no more wood chopping. It is significant that he stayed at Sparta for the stipulated four months and did not walk off the job.

Back in the Finger Lakes country, he attended school when

he could and picked up a rudimentary knowledge of arithmetic and geography. He somehow dug up the $2 to subscribe to a little circulating library and read its offerings at random. Conscious of his ignorance of the meaning of many of the words he read, he bought a small dictionary and studied it in his spare time. By his own account, he was 19 before he ever saw an atlas or a map or heard a sentence parsed.

It is a commentary on the rural educational system of the time that at 18 he was engaged to teach a district school at Scott. Rough boys had driven out the previous teacher. Whatever his scholastic deficiencies, the brawny Fillmore was able to enforce discipline. When one of the boys defied him and tried to grab a wooden poker, Fillmore seized the weapon and restored order. Then he gave the disturber a sound thrashing. Because he had brandished the poker, the school trustees called him on the carpet but he convinced them he was acting in self defense and he was allowed to complete the term.

After that he tended a saw mill for a time. Then in 1818 he set out, knapsack on his back, for a walk to Buffalo and return. His uncle was a Methodist preacher in the town on Lake Erie.

In later years when he was Buffalo's leading citizen, Millard Fillmore recalled his first sight of the straggling village, just rising from the ashes of the fire which the British soldiers had set in the War of 1812. He also remembered his blistered feet after the walk half way across the state.

In 1815 he became apprenticed to two cloth dressers at New Hope and contracted to work for them for six years for $55 a year. He went to school during slack times at the mill.

He managed to get in some schooling in 1818-1819 by boarding with a farmer and paying for his keep by chopping wood. This school was at Montville, a hamlet on the outskirts of Moravia, and its teacher was a tall, blue-eyed, queenly redhead named Abigail Powers. She was only two years Fillmore's senior.

She took an interest in the big, blonde, handsome lad who was struggling so hard to get "book learning." She helped with his studies after hours and they fell in love. But it was eight years before they could afford to marry.

Montville's leading citizen, the Quaker judge, Walter Wood, took a fancy to young Fillmore and offered him a chance to work and study law in his office. When he heard the offer, the young man sobbed for joy. He raised $30 to win release from his contract with the cloth dressers which had a year to run.

Mostly he served as an errand boy and copyist for Judge Wood but he kept his eyes and ears open and picked up a lot of legal information other than that he got from law books. He was not yet 21 when he was chosen to deliver the Fourth of July oration at the community celebration in the grove at Montville. He did so well that one citizen was heard to say: "That young man will be a judge some day."

A farmer who heard the oration was so impressed that he engaged Fillmore to plead a case for him in a peace justice court for a $3 fee. This action by his employe who had not yet been admitted to the bar displeased Judge Wood and he and Fillmore came to the parting of the ways.

In 1821 Fillmore left the Finger Lakes backwoods, where he had lived since birth, to join his family in their new home in East Aurora, Erie County. His horizon was widened in his new environment for East Aurora was only a few miles from Buffalo, now a flourishing village, fully recovered from the war raid, and soon to boom with the digging of the Clinton Ditch.

Fillmore's first years in Erie County were crowded ones. He read law in a Buffalo office while at the same time teaching school and serving as a postoffice assistant, sorting mail after school hours.

His industry was rewarded in 1823 when he was admitted to the practice of law in the Court of Common Pleas. The seven-year rule of study was waived in his case. Immediately he opened his own law office in East Aurora. Within a few years he was admitted to general state practice.

His eight-year courtship of Abigail Powers ended with their marriage in Moravia on Feb. 15, 1826, with the rector of St. Matthew's Episcopal Church tieing the knot.

Every whit as industrious as her husband, Abigail continued to teach after her marriage, even after the birth of their first child, Millard Powers, in 1828. She also taught herself French and the piano. Millard Fillmore had taken no ordinary country woman as his mate. And as long as she lived, he relied heavily on her counsel. They were a devoted couple. When apart, they wrote each other every day.

This pleasant-mannered, good-looking young lawyer was born for the political arena. In 1828 he made his debut as an active member of the new Anti Masonic Party, which was spawned by the disappearance of William Morgan. The Niagara Frontier, where Morgan was last seen alive, seethed with excitement.

At an Anti Masonic gathering in Buffalo, Fillmore met for the first time Thurlow Weed, an ambitious editor-Assemblyman from Rochester, who was using the Anti-Masonic movement as a springboard to personal political power. Weed, like Fillmore, had been born in dire poverty on the frontier. He saw great political promise in the young lawyer and groomed him for the State Assembly. Fillmore ran and was elected as an Anti Mason.

He served three terms in Albany. Among the measures he sponsored was one ending imprisonment for debt and another giving persons who professed no religious belief the right to testify in the courts.

When the Anti-Masonic movement faded, Weed steered Fillmore into the new Whig party, along with another protege, Senator William Henry Seward of Auburn. The three men were to loom large in state and national politics for 30 years.

As Weed rose steadily to state control, Fillmore became his chief lieutenant in Western New York. He was an excellent organizer, hard working and overlooking no details. He was not an eloquent speaker but his earnest, warm manner won his audiences. He had suave, ingratiating ways and he was cautious and guarded in his statements.

He had moved to the bustling town of Buffalo, had taken a law partner there and for the first time in his life had money in the bank. In 1832 he was a member of the committee that drew up Buffalo's first city charter. He was active in the Young Men's Lyceum and in the evenings taught an informal group of law students—gratis.

Although he always coyly pretended not to be seeking public office and seemed always to be "waiting for a draft," Fillmore at heart was intensely ambitious. Such a man was not to be out of public life for long.

In 1832 he was elected to Congress as a Whig. He served 10 competent, colorless years in the House, rising in 1842 to the chairmanship of the potent Ways and Means Committee. He followed the Whig party line faithfully, was diligent in the committee room and was considered a staunch antislavery legislator. He zealously looked after the interests of the Niagara Frontier and "ran errands" for his constituents. He sponsored "pork barrel" measures for local improvements and during the turbulence of the Canadian Patriot War demanded defense of the American border.

He fathered the tariff law of 1842 and was influential in getting the appropriation for a test of Morse's electric telegraph. He was a warm admirer of Henry Clay and a champion of the Kentuckian's expansive "American System."

So when his idol Clay seemed sure of the Whig nomination for the Presidency in 1844, Fillmore itched to be his running mate. Weed and Seward supported his candidacy —not too avidly—but the nomination went to another. Fillmore was rejected because it was feared his anti-slavery views might repel the Southern Whigs. The bosses need not have been so apprehensive. The Southern Whigs, in the end, had no firmer friend than Millard Fillmore. Anyhow, it did matter in 1844. The Whigs lost.

Weed salved Fillmore's disappointment by giving him the New York gubernatorial nomination that year. The boss figured that Fillmore's exemplary private life and his popularity in the rural "Bible-belts" might offset the stories of Clay's drinking, gambling and other peccadillos.

Fillmore, who yearned to be governor, found he had formidable opposition. For the Democrats had persuaded one of their ablest leaders, Silas Wright, to resign his Senate seat to make the run for governor. Fillmore was defeated by 10,000 votes and Clay lost New York by 5,000. The Liberty Party (abolitionist) ticket drew off many Whig votes. In a letter to Clay after the election, Fillmore blamed the result on "abolitionists and foreign Catholics."

After 1844 Fillmore's relations with Weed and Seward deteriorated but there was no open break. Fillmore's friends told him that Weed and Seward had hardly gone all out for him in the campaign and he wondered if his old allies wanted to sidetrack him. He wrote Francis Granger "he was not willing to be killed by pretended kindness."

Fillmore had always liked the bluff Weed, whose background was so like his own, and he respected the boss's political sagacity. But he resented Weed's eternal pushing of his crony, Seward, over all other Whigs—particularly over Millard Fillmore.

With Seward he had little in common. They were antithetical types. Fillmore was dignified, composed, cautious, deliberate, close mouthed, courtly. Seward was jumpy, theatrical, impulsive, tart tongued but charming when needs be.

It is possible that the self-made, self-taught Fillmore, a proud and sensitive man under the bland facade, was jealous of Seward's superior education, intellect and sophistication. He distrusted the Auburnian's sincerity and disagreed with many of his policies, notably his efforts while governor to extend equal educational opportunities to the foreign born in New York City. As for Seward he regarded his fellow Whig with an amused condescension. He did not conceal his low opinion of Fillmore's intellectual capacity.

Weed forced Fillmore to take the state comptrollership in 1847 and the Buffalonian resented being tossed so small a crumb. But the 1848 national election lay ahead and maybe the Vice Presidential lightning would strike him this time. He knew he would not have the support of the Weed machine and he made cautious alliances with its opponents.

Weed was out for bigger game. He essayed the Warwick role and scanning the field for Presidential timber, came up with Gen. Zachary Taylor, the popular hero of the Mexican War. The New York boss got the Taylor bandwagon rolling early and had much to do with the nomination of "Old Rough and Ready" for the Presidency over the perennial aspirant, Henry Clay, Fillmore's choice.

Weed's cup of bliss got a liberal dose of wormwood when an old enemy, John Collier of Binghamton, in a surprise move eloquently demanded the nomination of Millard Fillmore as Vice President to conciliate the defeated Clayites. The convention took to the idea and Weed had to go along —with misgivings.

However, he worked closely with Fillmore in the campaign. The Vice Presidential nominee lent strength to the ticket in the North but had to softpedal his anti-slavery record when courting the Southern Whig vote. With Van Buren heading a bolting Free Soil movement, the Democrats were divided and Taylor and Fillmore rode handily to victory.

Before they were inaugurated, Weed cracked the whip over a docile state legislature and William Seward went to the United States Senate. The partners wanted to be in on the ground floor of the new regime.

On March 4, 1849, Millard Fillmore took the oath as Vice President. His Abigail was not there for the ceremony. She was ailing and during her husband's tenure as Vice President remained at home in Buffalo, in the white house with the green blinds on Franklin Street.

Fillmore was a competent presiding officer. His years in Congress had given him a knowledge of parliamentary law. He was dignified, urbane, conciliatory, dispassionate and judicial.

And he certainly looked the presiding officer role. Handsome, smooth shaven, pink cheeked with sparkling blue eyes and carefully combed graying locks, with no excess of flesh on his big, impeccably clad, five foot, nine inch frame, he was an impressive figure in the chair.

Actually he was only a figurehead. This run-of-the-mill politician presided over the most glittering galaxy of Senatorial giants in history. He heard the oratorical thunder of Clay, Webster and Calhoun, the great triumvirate, in the twilight of their careers, but still magnificent. And there were superior younger leaders coming to the fore, such as Stephen A. Douglas of Illinois and Fillmore's New York rival, the brilliant Seward.

It was Fillmore's lot to referee part of the Great Debate of the time. It arose over the compromise measures proposed by Clay to ward off threats of sectional disunion over slavery in the wake of the Mexican War which added new territory. Feelings ran high in that turbulent, divided Senate over which Fillmore presided with tact and patience. When things got out of hand, he delivered a mild lecture on deportment. It was not too effective.

The Taylor administration was cool toward the Compromise. Fillmore favored it and went to the White House to tell the President that in case of a tie, he would vote for the measure.

Fillmore's futile tug of war with Weed and Seward for the President's favor and the New York patronage has been described in a previous chapter. Seward's acid comment on his victory was: "The Vice President is too dull of comprehension to understand what had happened."

Fillmore knew what had hit him all right and he retaliated by trying to build his own organization in New York and starting a paper in opposition to Weed's *Journal*.

Weed and Seward were in the clover patch. Fillmore was outside the pasture fence.

Then on July 9, 1850, old Zachary Taylor stood too long in the hot sun during the dedication of the Washington Monument, then ate too many sour cherries and drank too many glasses of cold milk. In a few hours he was dead of a fever, and Millard Fillmore, who had been only a figurehead, became the 13th President of the United States.

Immediately the whole Washington picture was changed. The Compromisers, with the vigorous Douglas taking the leadership from the tired old Clay, pushed their measures through. To the horror of his old anti-slavery friends, Fillmore signed them all, including a new and drastic fugitive slave law. That cost him support of the extremists in both North and South and led to his political downfall.

He and the other Compromisers sincerely believed they had averted what Seward was to call "an irrepressible conflict." They had merely postponed it a few years. The fires of sectionalism smouldered. They had not been quenched. Thousands at the North had no intention of obeying the new fugitive slave law.

Furthermore the Compromise paved the way for the Kansas-Nebraska Act which united the North behind the new Republican party and doomed the Whig party. The provisions whereby new territories "were to be admitted with or without slavery as their constitutions may prescribe" led to "Bleeding Kansas" and the madness of John Brown.

Fillmore never saw slavery as a moral issue. To him it was purely a political question. He stated his belief that "all unsolicited interference with slavery from other states and other countries will but aggravate the evil." He favored gradual emancipation and colonization. A recommendation he made in his third annual message for colonizing the Negroes in Africa or the West Indies was suppressed.

Within 10 days after taking office, Fillmore had tossed out the whole Taylor cabinet. Daniel Webster headed the new setup as secretary of state and Nathan K. Hall, Fillmore's longtime Buffalo law partner, was the new postmaster general. With Hall ladling out the patronage, Weed, Seward & Co. fared ill indeed.

After the Compromise crisis, Fillmore's reign was relatively uneventful. A general prosperity stifled radicalism. Fillmore was criticized for making Brigham Young, the Mormon leader, governor of Utah territory. When Louis Kossuth visited the White House, the President received him graciously but skillfully avoided any commitment. An outstanding event of the administration was the Perry naval expedition which opened Japan to world commerce.

An air of serenity pervaded the White House. Its master was a perfectly adjusted man. He did not smoke or drink and seemed to have no nerves. He once remarked that the only night's sleep he missed in his life was when Taylor's unexpected death confronted him with the highest office in the land.

Mrs. Fillmore was far from robust and their talented daughter, Mary Abigail, often acted as official hostess. The Fillmore son, Powers, was his father's secretary. There were no guests or parties at the White House on Sunday. The first family attended church religiously. During the Fillmore regime, the White House got its first library and its first bath tub, a zinc affair. The President accepted a silver mounted harness for his carriage horses from friends and there was no Congressional investigation.

Historians have generally agreed that Fillmore was a fourth rate President. In *The People's Choice,* journalist Herbert Agar was particularly unkind. He wrote:

"Fillmore would have been an nonentity in any period of history but during the crisis of 1850 he was so overshadowed as to be indiscernible. . . . The most interesting thing Fillmore ever did was to refuse the degree of doctor of civil law from Oxford University on the ground that he had no literary or scientific attainments."

Fillmore's son inexplicably directed in his will that all his father's papers be destroyed. Those letters and speeches that survive are revealing. In them there is no sparkle, no style, no words that echo through the years. There are plenty of glittering generalities, cautious verbiage, ambiguities, coy hints of availability for office while not openly seeking it. Through all the papers, one thread runs clearly. That is Fillmore's veneration for the Constitution. It motivated nearly all his official acts.

Bartlett's Quotations includes only two Fillmore sentences, both taken from his third annual message:

"Let us remember that revolution does not always establish freedom."

"It is not strange that such an exuberance of enterprise should cause some individuals to mistake change for progress and the invasion of the rights of others for national prowess and glory."

Neither as an orator or as master of deathless prose was Fillmore a Lincoln or a Wilson.

As his term drew to an end, Fillmore wanted renomination but he was too experienced a politician to have much hopes of attaining it. His signing of the fugitive slave law had alienated the "Wooly Heads," the anti-slavery wing of the party. Seward and Weed held the big New York bloc of votes against him. Only the Southern Whigs were in the President's corner.

Secretary of State Webster was an active candidate, too. Had the Webster and Fillmore forces combined their strength at the Baltimore convention, one or the other might have won. But the Southerners would have none of Webster. The North was set against Fillmore. Besides the vengeful

Seward was on the scene, marshalling votes for Gen. Winfield Scott, who finally won on the 53d ballot.

Fillmore took no part in the campaign which ended with the crushing defeat of Scott by Franklin Pierce. The Whig Party was to all intents and purposes dead.

The Fillmores had planned a Southern tour after leaving the White House but the frail Mrs. Fillmore suffered a chill during the bleak Pierce inaugural ceremony. She died in Willard's Hotel on March 30, 1853. The bereaved former President's thoughts must have turned back to a little country schoolhouse and a tall, auburn haired teacher helping an apprentice boy with his lessons. Abigail had been "eight years my sweetheart" and "27 years my wife," and he had never made an important decision without consulting her.

Fillmore was in Europe in 1856 when the American (Know Nothing) Party nominated him as its candidate for the Presidency. A forerunner of the Ku Klux Klan, this secret order got its nickname from the invariable reply of its members when questioned about the organization: "I know nothing."

The Know Nothings advocated a 21-year residence before naturalization, restriction of immigration, exclusion of Roman Catholics and the foreign born from office. Prejudice was rife against the Irish and Germans who had settled by the thousands in the big cities.

Fillmore was not a member of this nativist party, never attended any of its meetings nor did he by word or deed indicate that he favored its program. Yet he accepted its nomination.

The remnants of the Whig Party endorsed the Know Nothing ticket. The Democrats ran James Buchanan. The glamorous explorer, John C. Fremont, carried the standard of the Republican Party in its first national campaign. Of that newcomer among political parties, Fillmore said:

145

"We see a political party from the Free States alone. Can they have the madness or folly to believe that our Southern brethren would submit to such a chief magistrate? I tell you we are treading on the brink of a volcano."

The Know Nothings hoped by their crusade "for purity of American institutions" to draw attention from the seething controversy over slavery.

In the election Fillmore got 874,534 votes or 21.57 percent of the total cast and carried only the state of Maryland. Buchanan won decisively but the new Republican party had shown great strength.

Millard Fillmore's long political career was over. He devoted himself to his law practice and to civic affairs in Buffalo. He had been one of the founders of the University of Buffalo in 1846 and for 28 years until his death he was its chancellor. He was the first president of the Buffalo Historical Society, a founder of the Young Men's Association which became the Public Library; a founder of the Fine Arts Academy, the first president of the Buffalo Club, president of the General Hospital, trustee of Grosvenor Library. No public man ever participated more whole heartedly in the affairs of his community.

In 1858 Fillmore married Mrs. Caroline McIntosh, widow of a rich Albany merchant and the couple moved into an elegant eight-year old residence on Niagara Square, a pseudo Gothic miniature castle with all the trimmings and with tall poplars guarding its Delaware Avenue side. There the Fillmores entertained lavishly. Also they attended the Episcopal Church.

When the nation stood on the brink of the civil war Fillmore believed his signing of the Compromise bills had made impossible, the former President, with other oldline Whigs, supported the moderate Constitutional Union ticket of Bell and Everett.

After Lincoln was elected and the war came, Fillmore supported the Union although he considered many of Lincoln's emergency measures arbitrary and unconstitutional. He always believed the conflict could have averted with more patience on the part of the government.

In a Union rally in Buffalo at which he made the first subscription to a fund for soldiers, he proclaimed: "Our Constitution is in danger and we must defend it." It is significant he said "constitution," not "union." He was chairman of the Buffalo Defense Committee and commander of the Continentals, a home guard ceremonial outfit that escorted departing soldiers to trains and paraded on patriotic occasions. He made a truly splendid figure in his regimentals, with epaulets, sword, sash, brass buttons and plumed hat. There were those who considered Mr. Fillmore a little vain.

He also was an imposing civilian figure on the streets of Buffalo, in his black broadcloth suit, Prince Albert coat, tall hat and gold-headed cane. He greeted his fellow citizens with urbane, dignified courtesy.

He was Buffalo's official host to visiting dignitaries and entertained three Presidents. John Quincy Adams, an old Congressional comrade, came in 1843. In 1861 Lincoln, bound for his first inaugural, stayed overnight with the Fillmores and they all went to the Unitarian service the next day. In 1869 Fillmore was host to another President, Andrew Johnson.

Fillmore voted for McClellan, in 1864, hoping that a victory for the Democrat might end the war. He wanted the Union maintained without further bloodshed. He was still living in an age of compromise and appeasement that had passed with Clay and Webster.

Although he was Buffalo's most eminent citizen, his views made him unpopular with many of his fellow townsmen amid the tension and sufferings of a long war. Some had never forgiven him for signing the fugitive slave act which sent hundreds of Western New York Negroes fleeing into Canada. And during the war there hovered above the Niagara Frontier the threat of a rebel invasion from Canada. Such a thing was improbable but it kept the people on edge.

After news of Lincoln's assassination swept the city, a mob smeared Fillmore's house because no mourning was displayed. The former President explained that his wife was ill and he did not know his residence was undraped. The crowd only hooted at him.

After the war passions had died away, Buffalo showed affection and respect for its most distinguished citizen. Both he and his mansion were pointed out proudly to visitors. The ex-President kept up his interest in civic and cultural affairs and was on the platform at all public functions.

He had always been a friend of the Indians and in 1872, when he was old and failing, he took part in the last council fire of the Seneca Nation, held in the old Indian council house on the Glen Iris estate of his friend, William Pryor Letchworth, in what is now Letchworth State Park. Fillmore presented a medal to each Indian present. Among them were descendants of Red Jacket, Cornplanter and Joseph Brant.

While he was shaving on Feb. 13, 1874, he suffered a stroke of apoplexy. He died on March 8. His body lay in state in St. Paul's Cathedral and President Grant headed the notables who attended the funeral. Fillmore was buried in Buffalo's Forest Lawn Cemetery, along with Red Jacket and other greats of the Niagara Frontier.

Among the eulogistic obituaries in the nation's newspapers,

a frank "off-beat" note crept into the *Rochester Democrat* which said of the former President: "Intellectually he was substantial rather than brilliant."

History has not been kind to Millard Fillmore. To one historian he was a "bland nonentity." To another he was "a vain, handsome mediocrity." On the other hand Fillmore's biographer, Griffis, puts his subject on a pedestal with Lincoln, but one "who must wait for the slow justice of time." The historian Rhodes summed up neatly: "He was temperate, industrious, orderly and honest."

Those are the traits of a good citizen and Fillmore was that—if little more. Certainly he was ornamental. Queen Victoria is supposed to have called him the handsomest man she had ever seen.

Old neighbors in Buffalo liked to recall some of his kindly, courtly acts. For instance back in 1848, when a huge iron basket was suspended across the Niagara Gorge while a bridge was being built, Miss Jane Redfield, the adventurous daughter of a prominent Batavia family, wanted to ride in it. The gallant Fillmore would not allow her to go alone and insisted on taking the ride with her. The basket today is in the possession of the Buffalo Historical Society.

And there was the time when Fillmore and his first wife were invited to a social gathering not far from their home. Mrs. Fillmore had picked a corsage from the garden but left it at home. After her husband noticed it was missing he slipped quietly out of a side door, went home and fetched the bouquet. A little thing but characteristic of the man.

Fillmore may be the "forgotten President" in national history. But he is not forgotten in the region of his nativity and in the city where he lived so many years.

A state historical marker stands on the hard-to-find site of his birthplace on lonely Fillmore Road in the Cayuga County hills. Oats grow where stood the log cabin in which the baby Millard slept in a sap trough.

Nearby is the picturesque 400-acre Fillmore Glen State Park. There's a plaque on the wall of the interior of St. Matthew's Episcopal Church in Moravia stating that "Millard Fillmore and Abigail Powers were married in this parish."

Another plaque on the exterior wall of the big Hotel Statler on Buffalo's Niagara Square marks the site of the Fillmore mansion, which became a hotel and was remodeled at the time of the 1901 Pan-American Exposition into the Castle Inn. At the entrance to Buffalo's City Hall is a statue of Millard Fillmore, along with one of the city's other President, Grover Cleveland.

Fillmore Avenue is a principal Buffalo street. In the city also are the Millard Fillmore Hospital and Millard Fillmore College of the University of Buffalo. A village in Northern Allegany County bears the name of the 13th President.

He may not have been the greatest of our Presidents but he was the only one born in Central-Western New York.

Chapter 11

Raymond of the Times

Henry Jarvis Raymond was a farm boy from Lima who "made good in the Big Town."

He went far and he went fast. While still a young man, he was a power in journalism and in politics. He founded the *New York Times,* and the nation's foremost newspaper still hews to the course he set for it more than 100 years ago. He was one of the fathers of the Associated Press. He was a facile writer, a good reporter, an editor who got to the root of every matter.

He also was a founder of the Republican party, served in the state and national legislatures, as lieutenant-governor of New York and as Lincoln's campaign manager in 1864. He was an orator of renown. He was something of a scholar. He also was something of a playboy and his end was tragic.

He was born on Jan. 24, 1920, on an 80-acre farm in the rolling Genesee Country a mile from the village of Lima. His father, Jarvis Raymond, was of New England stock, a pillar of the Presbyterian Church and a holder of minor town offices.

His boyhood in Western New York was exceptional in that he seemed to prefer books to outdoor pastimes. It was said he could read at the age of three and at four years was going to the nearby district school. Next he attended the grade school in the village and when the Genesee Wesleyan Seminary opened on its hill above Lima in 1832, Henry Raymond was one of the 230 boys in its first class. He spent three years at the Seminary, which in 1869 became the cradle of Syracuse University.

For a short time he clerked in a country store, a job not to his liking. Within a year after leaving the Seminary, he was teaching the winter term of a district school in Wheatland and "boarding around" at farmhouses.

The short, slender, almost frail looking youth with the hazel eyes, olive complexion and large shapely head had gracious manners and was always impeccably attired. Along with bookish tastes and a flair for words, he was possessed of an insatiable ambition.

He determined to obtain a college education as one step toward the success he craved and September of 1836 found him on his way to Burlington and the University of Vermont. The family farm had been mortgaged to pay his college expenses.

At Vermont he distinguished himself as an orator and a writer. He sent verses to Horace Greeley's first newspaper, the *New Yorker,* and some of them were printed. He met Greeley in Albany, corresponded with the editor and in 1840 he got his first newspaper job on the *New Yorker.* He was put in charge of the literary department.

In the meantime, although he was not yet of voting age, he went back to his native county to campaign for Harrison and Tyler. He spoke at "Log Cabin" rallies in Lima, Geneseo and other towns.

When Greeley founded his penny paper, the *New York Tribune,* on a shoestring in 1841, he hired Raymond as his chief assistant. The young man worked hard, developed a facile writing style and soon he was reporting national events.

He began the study of law in a New York office on the side and became acquainted with some of the city's leading journalists and politicians.

Raymond parted company with Greeley after three years with the eccentric editor. He was innately conservative and abhorred most of the fads Greeley so eagerly espoused. Especially he differed with Greeley over the Fourierist Socialistic movement, whose chief disciple was Albert Brisbane, son of a Genesee County pioneer. Greeley went all out for the Utopians.

In 1843 Raymond took the editorship of the *Courier and Enquirer,* a Whig journal catering to the business community. The paper was owned by a colorful politician, Col. Jame Watson Webb. That same year the young editor married Juliette Weaver, whom he had met when he was a student in Vermont.

Raymond soon made a name for himself in the newspaper world. He became closely allied with the Whig leaders of the state, Thurlow Weed and William H. Seward. He wrote strong anti-slavery editorials. He played an important part in founding the co-operative newspaper alliance, the Associated Press, which began with six New York papers.

In the midst of the Taylor Presidential campaign which he supported with pen and voice, he was called home to Lima. The house in which he had been born was devoured by fire and he went to the aid of his parents who had mortgaged their farm to send him to college.

In 1850 he was elected to the State Assembly, as a Whig. A freshman member, barely 30 years old, he commanded attention because of his oratorical powers and his political know-how. In his second year he was elected Speaker. As a legislator he advocated a free school system and equal opportunity for all, often referring eloquently to his own rural boyhood.

His growing intimacy with Weed and Seward irritated Colonel Webb, who was serving in a diplomat post abroad, and their differences became so sharp that Raymond left the *Courier*.

For some time he and another young newspaperman, George Jones, had talked of starting a new paper in New York. They raised $40,000, sold stock and obtained "an angel" in E. B. Wesley of Albany. So on Sept. 17, 1851, the first issue of the *New York Daily Times* rolled off gleaming new Hoe "Lightning" presses in a six-story modern plant.

Raymond took the editorial helm and as long as he lived, he WAS the *New York Times*. He established it as a conservative newspaper, Whig in politics, but not blindly partisan. He steered for it a middle course between the reformist extremes of Greeley's *Tribune* and the sensationalism of Bennett's *Herald*.

He sought to make his paper an authoritative organ on economic and foreign affairs and sent skilled correspondents wherever news was breaking. He sensed that news was the core of any newspaper, and he chronicled the gay social doings at Saratoga, as well as financial and political affairs. He induced political leaders to contribute articles. He was indefatigable and his own pen was seldom idle. As a boss he was demanding but never dictatorial, and he stood by what his men had written even when it was contrary to his own views.

Raymond had a logical mind that saw all sides of an issue, a trait that sometimes hampered him in the political rough and tumble. And despite his mixing in practical politics, to the last he remained something of a blue stocking—an "egg head," he would be called today.

When Boss Weed threw the public printing to Raymond, Greeley was incensed. He satirized his slight, young rival as "Young Master Raymond." Later he called him "that young villain." Raymond disliked personalities but he fought back —and he had a pungent pen.

In 1854 the Whigs nominated for governor the temperance advocate, Myron H. Clark of Canandaigua. As Clark's running mate they chose Henry J. Raymond, no teetotaler. Greeley was outraged. He had wanted the lieutenant governorship himself. He sensed that Raymond was crowding him out of the Weed inner circle and getting all the plums.

Clark and Raymond won the election by narrow margins and the editor returned to Albany, to preside over the State Senate. He had much to do with the re-election of Seward to the United States Senate.

When the Republican party was being organized in New York State, Raymond was on the ground floor. He renounced his allegiance to the Whigs before Seward or Weed did. He was against slavery but he was not an abolitionist. He drafted a declaration of principles for the new party's national convention that led to his being called the "godfather of the Republican party."

In 1859 the editor of the *Times* visited the Italian front in the Franco-Austrian war and sent back exclusive reports of the fighting. In the tempest over the slavery issue at home he called for concessions on both sides and for the preservation of the Union. He cautioned against the Republicans taking too radical a position and he saw back of the secession movement the South's fear of its loss of political power.

Raymond went to the Republican convention of 1860 in Chicago as an adherent of his friend, Seward. He strove to offset Greeley's vengeful work against Seward among the delegates. When Lincoln won the nomination, the disappointed Raymond sulked a while, then swung vigorously to the cause of the gaunt nominee from Illinois.

Amid the thickening war clouds in the wake of Lincoln's election, Raymond appealed to the moderates in the South to stick with the Union. But the time for compromise had passed. After the Civil War broke out, Raymond was at Bull Run and wrote an eye-witness account of the Union debacle.

With his friend, Leonard W. Jerome, a stockholder in the *Times*, he went to the front during McClellan's snail-like advance on Richmond and the pair saw some of the fighting of the Seven Days. Jerome, a stock market plunger and flamboyant sportsman, came from Upstate New York and had published a newspaper in Rochester. He and Raymond had kindred tastes. Leonard Jerome is remembered today only because his daughter married Lord Randolph Churchill and bore a son named Winston.

During the draft riots in New York, Raymond mounted two Gatling guns in the *Times* office, manned one himself, with Jerome taking charge of the other. The mob they expected did not come.

Raymond drove himself at a furious pace during the war. He was much in Washington, conferring with the President and other leaders. Generally his paper defended Lincoln's policies although he did not hesitate to criticize on occasion. He paid his war correspondents well and his coverage of the conflict was as good, if not better, than his rivals. The *Times* grew in prestige and circulation, and its editor rose with it.

In 1864, after dashing off a history of Lincoln's first term, for campaign purposes, Raymond was chosen to manage the President's bid for re-election. He also was made chairman of the National Committee of the Union Party, the Republican label being dropped for that election. Lincoln's success is generally credited to the Union's military victories in the Fall.

Raymond got himself elected to Congress that year—by a scant 500 votes. In the House he championed the administration and after the death of Lincoln, he was just as staunch in his support of the Johnson policies. Consequently he was at odds with the Radical bloc, led by Thaddeus Stevens, who wanted the South treated as a conquered province. Raymond outshone Stevens in oratory but he was no match for the club-footed Pennsylvanian in political tactics. The two men were personally friendly. Few men—or women—could resist Raymond's charm.

Raymond's stands in Congress were often inconsistent, because of his tendency to look at all sides of a matter. As a politician he was colorful but not always effective.

In 1866 he sealed his political doom by taking a prominent part in the Union convention, a strange gathering of former Rebels, Copperheads, Union Democrats and followers of Andrew Johnson. The dominant Radicals in the Republican party ousted Raymond as national chairman. He did not seek re-election to Congress, knowing he would be defeated. In 1868 he bolted the Johnson camp and went back into the Republican ranks, his influence departed.

Henry Raymond's Presbyterian father would not have approved of his son's private life, especially after his political decline. The engaging little editor with the elegant side whiskers and the fine raiment became a familiar figure in the night life of New York. His wife was seldom seen with him. Prim Juliette Raymond, out of Vermont, shared none of her husband's worldly tastes. She detested the theater and cards. Besides she had a violent temper and although Raymond was of sunny nature, they had many quarrels. Mrs. Raymond and their children spent considerable time abroad.

The debonair journalist's detours down the primrose path caused talk along Broadway, especially his intimacy with the reigning favorite of the stage, dark-eyed Rose Eytinge.

Raymond's health began to fail before he was 50. His eyes troubled him, his hands trembled and he developed a twitch of the facial muscles. Although his political career was over, he still worked long hours at the *Times* office. The newspaper was his real love.

On the night of June 18, 1869, a carriage pulled out in front of the Raymond home in New York. Two men, supporting a third, got out. The third man was Raymond. His drinking companions, thinking their friend had merely "passed out," deposited the sagging body on the floor and went away.

Raymond's daughter, Mary, heard her father's labored breathing and summoned a doctor. Henry Raymond had suffered a stroke and before dawn the founder of the *New York Times*, the Lima farmboy who had scaled the heights, was dead.

Chapter 12

Governors Four

Western New York can hardly be called "the mother of governors." Of the 44 elected chief executives of New York only 10 came from the western part of the state. In this century there has been but one, Frank W. Higgins of Olean, elected in 1904.

There was a time, however, when this region was not so overshadowed by the Big Town and the downstate political powers. Between 1847 and 1865 no less than four governors were elected from this end of the state.

Those governors were:

John Young of Geneseo, who served from 1847 to 1849, a Whig who rode into office as the champion of the Anti-Renters.

Washington Hunt of Lockport, (1851-1853) another Whig, who owed his political success to his fence-straddling ability.

Myron H. Clark of Canandaigua (1855-1857), idol of the "drys," a Whig whose endorsement by the prohibitionists gave him his margin of victory.

Reuben E. Fenton of Jamestown, (1865-1869), a Radical Republican, the only two-termer of the four and the only one to become state leader of his party.

*   *   *

John Young was a self-made man whose beginnings were humble. Born in Chelsea, Vt., in 1802, an only child, he came to Livingston County at the age of four. His father, Thomas Young, ran a tavern at Conesus before turning to farming.

The future governor went to district school and to the Lima Academy and at the age of 16 was teaching school in Conesus for $9 a week. After reading law in an East Avon office, he was admitted to the bar and hung out his shingle in the shire town of Geneseo.

He was persuasive with a jury and soon was recognized as an effective trial lawyer. He was a six footer with keen eyes and was clean shaven save for a short tuft of beard under his chin. His impressive appearance was marred by a chronic tilt of his head to the left, a condition caused by rheumatism.

Young entered politics at the age of 28 as an unsuccessful Democratic candidate for county clerk. He switched to the Anti-Masonic Party and in 1831 was elected to the State Assembly on that ticket. After one term in Albany, he returned to public life in 1836 as a Whig Congressman and served until 1843. He attracted no particular attention either in the Assembly or in Congress in those years.

In 1844 John Young went back to the Assembly. It was there in the 1845-46 session that he leaped from obscurity to party leadership. With skill and tact he led the Whig minority in championing a convention for revision of the State Constitution and by a coalition with the Hunker (conservative) Democrats, he forced through the necessary legislation.

The tall lawyer was as convincing in caucus or on the floor of the Assembly as he had been before a Genesee Valley jury. He kept his Whigs in line while he made shrewd combinations with whichever wing of the divided Democracy suited his purposes in driving Whig measures through. He held his own in debate with the rising Democratic leader, Horatio Seymour.

John Young's star rose swiftly. Alexander, the historian of New York politics, calls him "a one-season comet." He made his reputation in one session of the Legislature. In that session he engineered legislation for expansion of the Genesee Valley and Black River Canals, projects dear to the rural voters' hearts. His smartest political move was his espousing the cause of the Anti-Renters, the embattled farmers of the Hudson Valley who had challenged the patroons.

At first a localized struggle, it was fanned into a full-blown revolt against a feudal system of leasehold tenure in 1845 when an undersheriff was slain at an eviction sale. The Democratic Governor, Silas Wright, declared Delaware County in a state of insurrection and sent in the militia to quell the uprising. The Anti-Renters developed political consciousness and in 1846 were in a position to reward their friends and punish their enemies.

So after the Democrats had renominated the able Governor Wright, who had put down the revolt, John Young, champion of the Anti-Renters, was a formidable candidate for the Whig gubernatorial nomination. Thurlow Weed did not admire him. He made scathing comment about people mistaking cunning and diplomacy for intellectual power. But Weed did not have control of the Whigs that year. When he saw the drift toward Young, he left the convention in disgust. Young won the nomination on the third ballot. There were some votes for Millard Fillmore but the Buffalo politico did not want to run that year. Besides he was a friend of Young.

Young was elected governor by a margin of 11,000 votes. The Anti-Renters held the balance of power and they were

161

all for Young. Besides the Hunker Democrats knifed Silas Wright.

When word of Young's victory reached Geneseo, there were bonfires, the boom of cannon and a torchlight parade which wound up at the home of the Governor-elect in Second Street, the present residence of Mrs. Esther P. Campbell.

During the campaign there were charges that Young had made a deal with the Anti-Renters—to pardon their men convicted of murder in exchange for votes. At any rate, soon after he took office, the Governor released the men. The Anti-Rent war ended within a few years as the land barons, one by one, sold their holdings. It was a victory for grass roots democracy against an outdated, aristocratic system.

As Governor, Young did not display the qualities of leadership that had marked his legislative career. His ability was as a tactician and parliamentarian, rather than as an administrator. He did not seek renomination. Had he done so, it would have been useless, for the burly figure of Thurlow Weed stood in the way. The old boss was back in firm control.

When Zachary Taylor was elected President and two New York Whig factions, one led by Weed and Seward and the other by the new Vice President, Fillmore, struggled for patronage, Young stuck with Fillmore. The Vice President was able to reward him with the post of assistant United States treasurer, stationed in New York City.

John Young was holding that office when he died of tuberculosis in 1852 at the age of 50. He sleeps in the old Temple Hill Cemetery above Geneseo, in the Valley where he had been so popular.

*   *   *

Washington Hunt was the "boy wonder" of his time in politics and finance. He was a county judge at the age of 24, a member of Congress at 31 and governor of New York before he was 40. He made a fortune in land speculation before his 30th birthday.

For 30 years the political spotlight shone on him. He was a minor actor but an engaging one in most of his roles. Forever he was romping in from the wings, extending an olive branch or pouring oil on troubled waters. He was a congenital peacemaker, eventually to the cost of his reputation.

A picture of the 15th elected Governor of New York hangs on the wall of his old law office in Lockport, preserved as a part of the Niagara County Historical Center. There is something boyish and ingratiating about the smooth-shaven face, framed by wavy hair. The eyes are frank and friendly, the mouth is pleasant but the chin is as firm as a block of Lockport limestone. Hunt changed his political coat often but he never swerved from his chosen path of compromise—even when loyalty to the Union was involved.

He was born in Windham, Greene County, in 1811, of New England ancestry. His father, Sanford Hunt, after suffering financial reverses, sought a fresh start on the Genesee Country frontier. In 1818, with his wife and seven children, he settled in the wilds of the Town of Portage in Livingston County.

Sanford Hunt did well on the frontier. To his farm he added a store, a mill, an ashery. He became the principal citizen of the little settlement that was named for him, Hunt's Hollow. Now it is plain Hunts.

After young Washington had gone through the district school, he attended the Geneseo Academy, paying his tuition by working before and after classes. He got a job in a village store and when the merchant moved to the booming canal town of Lockport, his 17-year-old clerk went along. Lockport was to be the home of Washington Hunt the rest of his days.

He left the store to study law in Lot Clark's office. His rise was spectacular. Admitted to the bar in 1834, he was elected the first judge of Niagara County that same year—as a Van Buren Democrat. In 1833 he became associated with Henry Walbridge and other speculators in the Albany Land Company which had bought thousands of wild acres in Northwestern New York from the Holland Land Company. Hunt married Walbridge's daughter, Mary, in 1834. The land venture was vastly successful; the Erie Canal boomed the Niagara region and young Hunt rode the crest of the wave.

He bought a stately brick house on Market Street fronting the Erie Canal in Lockport's "Lower Town," and opened a law office nearby. He championed the interests of "Lower Town" against its rival on the hill, "Upper Town," now the principal business district of the City of the Locks.

"Lower Town" is rather run down these days but in the 1830s and 1840s it was a bustling place with stores, docks, a rambling, porticoed hotel beside the canal and elegant cutstone houses along Market Street. Hunt's old home is still there, with a sign "dressmaking" in an upper window and a historical marker which states that President Van Buren was a guest of Washington Hunt there in 1839.

As the two men sat on the porch of the brick house watching the passing parade of packets and barges on the Clinton Ditch, one wonders if the host told the President of his growing distaste for the administration's fiscal policies. At any rate when the next year found Hunt marching with the Harrison-Tyler Whigs, he gave that reason for deserting Van Buren. It was the first of his political flops.

Hunt had irons in many fires. Besides the law and the land agency, he was a bank president, the owner of local real estate, an insurance business and a cotton factory. He was interested in Lockport enterprises including the celebrated

Merchants Gargling Oil Company, as well as in Western land and railroads.

He was a pillar of Christ Episcopal Church in "Lower Town." He gave liberally to worthy causes. This busy man found time to pen this note, now in the archives of the Niagara County historian:

"Please give this boy a spelling book and I will pay for it—W. Hunt."

And he found time for politics, a field in which he could employ his talents for conciliation and compromise. In 1842 he was elected to Congress as a Whig. He served three terms. He followed the Whig line, voting for the Wilmot Proviso and against Texas annexation. He was a good speaker with a ready flow of words. He created no great stir in Congress but he made a lot of friends. In 1849 he was named state comptroller.

The 1850 state Whig convention was historic because of the split between the Weed-Seward forces and the followers of President Fillmore that culminated in the bolt of the "Silver Grays." Despite the bitterness, both sides agreed on the middle-of-the-road state comptroller, Washington Hunt, as their choice for governor. His policy of not taking sides paid off.

In the election Hunt defeated the Democrat, Horatio Seymour, by only 262 votes.

As governor, with the backing of Boss Weed, he pushed through a nine million dollar appropriation for the state waterways, an act ruled unconstitutional by the Court of Appeals within a year. He urged establishment of a state agricultural college and expressed concern over the number of immigrants arriving in New York. He failed to express concern over their welfare. And he labored valiantly and vainly to heal the rift between the two factions of his party.

In 1852 he revisited the scenes of his youth when he journeyed to Portage for the opening of the High Bridge of the Erie Railroad over the foaming falls.

Hunt was renominated for the governorship but 1852 was a year of Whig debacle in the state and in the nation. Hunt lost to Seymour by 22,000 while Pierce was snowing under the Whig presidential hope, Scott.

The former governor bought a Summer home on the outskirts of Lockport which he named Wyndham Lawn in honor of his birthplace. That estate now is the Children's Home, a community supported project. Hunt's stone mansion forms the central part of its main building and the stone lodge of the gate keeper still stands beside the highway.

There came a time when Hunt had to take sides on the slavery issue. He went into the Fillmore camp of compromisers. He deplored the growth of sectionalism and shunned the new Republican party, which raised its standard in New York in 1854. In 1855 he received a few votes for Senator but Seward won easily. In 1856 he supported Fillmore, the nominee of the dissolving Whigs and the "Know Nothings."

In a speech he made in December, 1859, Hunt revealed his "peace at almost any price" attitude. After denouncing John Brown's "scheme of murder and insurrection," he declared:

"Every patriotic heart must desire the restoration of mutual confidence . . . the constant discussion and agitation of the slavery question has become an intolerable nuisance."

The former governor, like Millard Fillmore, was strangely blind to the moral issue involved.

The momentous year of 1860 found Hunt presiding over the national convention of the Constitutional Union party, made up of die hard, compromise Whigs who nominated Bell and Everett. He had turned down a nomination for vice president on the Democratic ticket. In New York he joined with his old rival, Seymour, in a futile scheme to split the state electoral vote among Lincoln's three opponents.

Lincoln's victory sent Hunt back to his political first love, the Democratic party. He became a rabid anti-administration Democrat, constantly demanding a cessation of hostilities.

In 1863 a petition was sent from Lockport to the White House, asking President Lincoln to rescind his Emancipation Proclamation on the ground it spelled economic ruin for the South. Hunt's name headed the list of signers.

By then many of his neighbors, especially those who had given loved ones to the Union cause, had turned against Lockport's most famous citizen and the ugly tag of "Copperhead" was applied to Washington Hunt.

The low water mark of Hunt's career came in 1864 when he accompanied the Copperhead mayor of New York, Fernando Wood, to a conference with Confederate peace commissioners, at the Clifton House in Niagara Falls. One of the commissioners was the notorious Jacob Thompson, who had fomented several plots to spread disorder in the North. The meeting came to nothing. Hunt and Wood had no authority to negotiate.

Hunt was a delegate to the Democratic national convention of 1864. Two years later, although the mark of death was upon him, he went to the National Union convention, a mongrel gathering of the foes of the Radical Republicans. There Hunt and his old mentor, Thurlow Weed, were in the same political pew again.

Washington Hunt died in 1867 in New York where he had gone for treatment in his long battle against cancer. He was only 56. He sleeps in Lockport's Glenwood Cemetery in the shadow of a monument 22 feet high.

In 1955 his little brick law office was moved up the hill

from "Lower Town" to the Historical Center grounds on Niagara Street. The office has been restored in the manner of the 1830s. The desk at which Hunt sat as agent of the land company is there, along with some of his law books. In the yard is a sleigh which he once owned and in which he rode with DeWitt Clinton when it carried the first mail from Niagara Falls to Lockport. In the museum next to the law office are goblets and china that belonged to the Hunts.

Lockport honors the memory of the public servant who shed luster on the town in a happier time and has forgiven the "Copperhead" that Washington Hunt became when he followed strange trails in his passion for peace.

*   *   *

Myron H. Clark of Canandaigua was the only governor of New York who owed his election to the prohibitionist vote. He was the beneficiary of a transitory wave of dry sentiment that bobbed up in the 1850s. And as governor he signed the bill that made the Empire State bone dry—in theory at least—for 11 months.

He was no demagogue, this county seat merchant with the chin whisker and the keenly chiseled features. He was an ardent champion of Free Soil as well as prohibition, simply because he sincerely believed that both slavery and intemperance were evils. Never did he sacrifice his principles to political expediency.

Nor was he one of those hypocrites who were dry only in their public statements and voting. Witness this jingle which he wrote for a young grandson long after his term as governor:

> *"Rum and tobacco I always eschew*
> *And I respectfully commend same to you."*

He was born in Naples in 1806 of New England ancestry. His grandfather, a veteran of the Revolution, was an early settler in the Naples area. His father, a farmer and lumberman, volunteered in the War of 1812 and was captured by the British.

Myron went to the district school, lived the normal life of a boy on the frontier. He joined his father in running the farm and the saw mill and learned the cabinet-maker's trade. Early in life he became interested in politics, held minor local offices and in 1837 was elected sheriff of Ontario County as a Whig.

After his term ended he kept his residence in Canandaigua, where he opened a hardware store. He became a pillar of the shire town, a trustee of the Congregational Church and president of the village. He had a wide acquaintance in the region. Farmers and villagers who bought their nails, shovels, plow points at his store liked and respected the quiet, serene merchant, who had served three years as their sheriff.

In 1851 he was the successful Whig candidate for State Senator and was re-elected in 1853. In the Legislature he was identified with the "Wooly Heads," the wing of the party opposed to the extension of slavery and at odds with "the Silver Grays," who favored compromise and were led by Clark's fellow townsman, Francis Granger.

The Canandaigua Senator rose to the leadership of the temperance forces in the Legislature. A strong prohibitionist tide was rising. Maine had adopted a law which forbade the sale of intoxicants except for medicinal purposes. Clark headed the committee which reported out a similar bill for New York State and he steered it through both houses, only to have it killed by the resounding veto of the Democratic governor, Horatio Seymour.

Senator Clark strongly opposed the Kansas-Nebraska bill

which opened the way to slavery in the new territories and was a burning issue of the time. When New York sanctioned the consolidation of a network of competing Upstate railroad lines into the New York Central, Clark was influential in fixing the fare at two cents a mile, over the agonized protests of Dean Richmond, vice president of the system and a master lobbyist.

When the Whigs gathered in Syracuse in 1854 to select their state ticket, Clark, the darling of the drys, had the largest following. Horace Greeley hungered for the nomination for governor. Boss Thurlow Weed had no particular liking for Clark or his extreme dry views but he didn't want his old partner, Greeley, at the head of the ticket either. So he bowed to the current and Clark emerged the nominee.

The 1854 election was a mixed-up affair. The Free Soil and Prohibition conventions endorsed Clark. The divided Democrats had two candidates, Governor Seymour and Greene Bronson. The Native Americans (Know Nothings), in open alliance with "the Silver Grays," also had a ticket in the field.

Clark made no speeches in the campaign but stayed quietly in Canandaigua. He won by a slim margin of 309 votes over his nearest rival, Seymour. The dry vote had tipped the scales for Clark. His home town celebrated with a 100-gun victory salute and a banquet in the Canandaigua Hotel.

The Whig party was on its deathbed and the Governor and the elements which had supported him were drawn into the new-born Republican party. Myron Clark in later years liked to think of himself as the first Republican governor although he had not run under that label.

As Governor he supported and signed the same drastic prohibition legislation that Seymour had vetoed. New York State was officially bone dry for 11 months from April, 1855, to

March, 1856, when the Court of Appeals declared the act unconstitutional. The law had been openly flouted by saloonkeepers and enforcement agencies, especially in the cities.

Greeley gave the Clark regime the blessing of his potent *New York Tribune* and was rewarded with the state printing. That did not set well with Weed. The temperance tide was ebbing and Clark had no chance of being renominated. Weed bossed the 1856 Republican convention and dictated the choice of John A. King for governor.

Clark was to have another taste of public life. President Lincoln named him the first internal revenue collector for the Western New York district in 1862 but political influences forced him out during the second Lincoln term. He returned to Canandaigua to spend the rest of his days, living quietly in the gracious gray brick home, built in the colonial pattern, that still stands in Gibson Street.

When Clark was governor, young Frederick Ferris Thompson of New York, a son of the founder of the Chase National Bank, came to the Executive Mansion to court a Clark daughter, Mary. They were married in 1857. After her husband's death, Mrs. Thompson lived on an elaborate estate in Canandaigua, now the site of the Veterans Hospital. She became a sort of Lady Bountiful to the community, donating a hospital in her husband's memory, a playground and the site for the Postoffice.

Myron Clark lived to the good old age of 86. Old residents of Canandaigua recall the kindly old man who liked to watch ball games and to fish with a crony on Canandaigua Lake, wearing a linen duster and a broad-brimmed straw hat.

*   *   *

Reuben Fenton was "a politician's politician." He knew all the tricks of the trade and was as foxy as they came, always ready to make a deal or grant a favor. Chauncey M. Depew, a close observer of New York politics for more than half a century, called him "the greatest political organizer since Martin Van Buren."

This suave schemer, the first governor to hail from the Southern Tier, climbed the political ladder with calculated patience, from supervisor of a rural township to the United States Senate chamber. He had his hour of glory as Republican boss of the Empire State. He got his comeuppance when he clashed with an equally ambitious but more spectacular, more aggressive and more ruthless politician, Roscoe Conkling.

Fenton was not an accomplished orator. His talent was in the caucus and the committee room. A master wire puller, he built up a strong personal following and gradually a well oiled state machine.

The wealthy Chautauquan, who never ceased his pursuit of the golden fleece, looked the statesman. He was tall, erect, faultlessly groomed, with an impressive iron gray beard. He was every bit as genial to a farmer from the back country as to a political or financial bigwig.

Reuben Eaton Fenton was born in Carroll, Chautauqua County, on the 4th of July in 1819, a farmer's son. He received a better education than the average country youth of that period, for he attended a school near Cincinnati, as well as the nearby Fredonia Academy, which grew into the present State Teachers College.

He was admitted to the bar but soon deserted Blackstone for the marts of trade. At the age of 20 he opened a general store in Frewsburg. When he saw fortunes being made from the great pine forests of the Southern Tier, he jumped into the lumbering business. He piloted his first raft load of logs down the Allegheny and Ohio Rivers and sold it at a nice profit. It was not long before young Fenton was one of the most successful lumbermen of the region. He moved to Jamestown, the metropolis of the region, in 1863 and lived in style.

Before that he had served five terms as the Democratic supervisor of the Town of Carroll and had been a colonel of the local militia. In 1852 he was elected to Congress as a Democrat but two years later lost his seat to the "Know Nothing" candidate.

Fenton was an early convert to Republicanism and presided over the first state convention of the new party in 1855. The next year he was elected to the first of his four terms as a Republican Congressman from the same district he had represented as a Democrat. In Congress, under either label, he was strongly anti-slavery. He also was considered an authority on currency problems.

His friends proposed him for governor in 1862 but he was willing to wait. He was then firmly in the Republican Radical camp although he supported Lincoln's war policies. In 1864 he was in the running for the vice presidency but was glad to settle for the gubernatorial nomination. He defeated the Democratic incumbent, Seymour, by 8,220, running ahead of President Lincoln in the state.

By then the reins of power had slipped from Thurlow Weed's hands and Fenton became the acknowledged leader of the ruling Radical faction of the party. Carefully he cemented his position through patronage and won re-election to the governorship in 1866.

As governor, he demonstrated his talent for management. He favored a spending program for the canals but he was no foe of the railroads—or of any other business interest. A highlight of his regime was the establishment of Cornell as a state land grant university.

Fenton was unable to prevent the election of the rising Mohawk Valley orator, Roscoe Conkling, to the Senate in 1867. He realized the handsome, haughty new Senator would be a dangerous rival. But he was gearing his machine toward winning a Senate seat himself in 1869.

He manipulated the Legislature to that end and found himself in the Senate where Conkling was strutting to the music of his bombastic oratory, winning power through his majestic presence and the fear inspired by his savage, merciless tongue.

The two New York Senators waged an epic tug of war for the favor of President Grant and the federal patronage. In the end the silent soldier in the White House turned from the devious, unctuous Fenton and took to his political bosom the flamboyant Conkling who always fought in the open.

A showdown in the patronage war came in the Senate when Fenton opposed the confirmation of a Conkling vassal, one Thomas Murphy, for the rich prize of the collectorship of the port of New York. After Fenton had presented carefully documented charges against Murphy, his antagonist put on a typical Conkling show. A vivid account of the incident is contained in Donald Barr Chidsey's biography of Conkling, "The Gentleman from New York."

Striding to Fenton's desk, Conkling drew from his pocket a paper which he said was a court record, "the particulars of which I will not relate without a special request of my colleague." He waved the document in Fenton's face. The head of the junior Senator fell as if he had been struck with a broadaxe.

Fenton well knew the nature of that court record. Some years earlier he had been sent to Albany with a large sum of money and arrived to say he had lost it. He was arrested, examined and discharged. Still he did not want that bit of dirty linen hung in the Senate chamber. Conkling's cruel theatrical performance brought about the confirmation of Murphy by a wide margin. And Reuben Fenton's prestige had been struck a staggering blow.

At the 1870 state convention Senator Conkling dominated the delegates by the sheer force of his personality, routed the Fentonites and seized control of the state Republican party. His possession of the federal patronage was his trump card. Reuben Fenton was politically dead.

Because he had no other place to go, he turned up in the Liberal Republican camp, pulling wires for the nomination of his old ally, Horace Greeley. Fenton came back briefly into the news as a delegate to the International Monetary Conference in Paris in 1878.

In his home town, he remained Jamestown's first citizen, popular and respected. He kept close watch of his extensive business interests. His career "followed the script" to the end. The former Governor died of a heart attack while attending a meeting of bank directors in 1885.

Another native son, who also spent his youth at Frewsburg, bounded on to the national stage in the 1930s to challenge Fenton's hitherto undisputed place in local history as Jamestown Citizen No. 1. That was the New Deal's fair haired boy, the late Justice Robert H. Jackson.

Reuben Fenton is not forgotten in his home city. There's a statue of the bearded politico in the six-acre Fenton Memorial Park, which also houses the 32-room, three-story Fenton mansion, now a meeting place for veterans' organizations.

And in Jamestown the Governor Fenton Hotel was a leading hostelry for years. It now is an office building. Greater fame hath no politician than that a hotel—or a cigar—be named for him.

Chapter 13

The General from the Valley

The grandee of the Genesee Valley did not have to go to war and lose his life in the bloody tangle of the Wilderness. In the first place he was over the age for volunteers.

James Samuel Wadsworth had inherited one of the largest estates in America, thousands of rich acres along the Genesee. He was politically ambitious. He had manifold interests besides his many farms. And there was the gracious wife and the three young sons in the manor house he had built. He could have stayed at home and sat the war out or made his contribution to the Union in the bullet-proof field of "public service," as so many of his contemporaries did.

But that was not his way. Along with a vast fortune, he had inherited a fighting spirit and a love of freedom. He abominated human slavery. So he volunteered at the first call for arms and fought at the earliest major battle of the Civil War, Bull Run.

Patriotism was in his blood. One of his ancestors had saved the charter of Connecticut colony from a tyrannical royal governor by hiding it in a tree that was forever after known as the Charter Oak.

Wadsworths had fought for liberty in the Revolution. William Wadsworth, uncle of James S., had served on the Niagara Frontier as a general of militia in the War of 1812.

And before the Civil War ended, all of James S. Wadsworth's three sons were in Union blue.

This Wadsworth, who in the lore of the Valley will always be "the General," was born in Geneseo in 1807, the eldest son and the second of five children of James and Naomi Wolcott Wadsworth. His father and his bluff uncle Bill had taken a vast tract along the Genesee when it was wilderness. The pioneeering Connecticut Yankee brothers founded in the Valley of the Genesee a family fortune, a land-holding dynasty, the oldest existing tenant farm system in America and a way of life.

When baby James arrived at the Home Place, the ancestral seat that now is called the Homestead, his father not only was a very wealthy land owner but one whose influence in politics and business extended beyond the Genesee Valley. The elder James eschewed public office. His son, as we shall see, did not share that antipathy.

Born to the purple, young James S. attended Harvard but failed to get a degree. He was no student, but a man of action. He read law for a season in the Boston office of the great Daniel Webster, spent a year at Yale Law School (all the Wadsworths go to Yale), and studied law in an Albany office before being admitted to the bar. He never practiced but found his knowledge of law valuable in administering the family realm.

He came home in 1833 to take from the shoulders of his aging father most of the burden of managing the estate. The next year he married Mary Craig Wharton, 19, and a beauty, the daughter of a rich Philadelphia Quaker merchant.

During their honeymoon abroad, the young couple were enchanted with Lord Hartford's villa near London and in 1835 they built a replica of it in Geneseo. Stately Hartford

House, where four generations of Wadsworths have dwelt, is at the northern edge of the village, set well back from the highway and surrounded by massive oaks. It has a three-story central section, with two wings, and overlooks a fine view of the Valley to the Southward.

The three sons, Charles F., Craig W. and James Wolcott, destined to serve many terms in Congress and become master of Hartford House, were born there. The manor house in James S. Wadsworth's time knew some famous guests, among them Charles Sumner, "Prince John" Van Buren and titled British visitors.

In 1842 the senior James Wadsworth died at the Home Place. His brother, William, had passed on in 1833. J. S. Wadsworth followed the pattern set by his methodical, far-sighted father in managing the estate. He was more approachable and liberal than his rather reserved sire, who had coped with the frontier.

The career of the younger James was sprinkled with humane and generous acts. During the Irish famine of 1847, he sent a ship load of grain to the sufferers. When in the late 1850s the Valley wheat crop was ruined by blight and excessive rainfall, a blow which ended its prestige as "the Nation's Bread Box," he forgave the rent for some tenants and helped others get a fresh start in the West.

In December, 1850, the steamer Atlantic in which he was returning from his sister's wedding in London was crippled in stormy seas eight days out. The crew, aided by Wadsworth and other passengers, set the ice-bound sails and the ship finally made port safely in Cork, Ireland. Suspense was intense in the Valley until word came in February that Wadsworth was safe.

When he drove home from Rochester after his return from the perilous trip, the whole Valley was alight with bonfires. Bells rang and cannon thundered. The yeomen were not making a perfunctory feudal gesture in honor of the squire. The freemen of the Genesee Valley had a genuine affection for their distinguished neighbor.

Wadsworth had extensive real estate interests in many places. But he never lost interest in his own region. He was active in promoting a railroad through the Valley and became the first president of the Rochester & Genesee Valley Railroad which in 1854 began operating from Rochester to Avon. It eventually became a part of the Erie system.

He was the first president of the State Agricultural Society and brought a Kentucky bull to the Valley to improve the breed. He was a regent of the State University and fought to locate a Normal School in Geneseo. That battle was won after his death.

His father had been a Whig but James S. Wadsworth joined the anti-slavery wing of the Democratic party, led by former President Martin Van Buren. Wadsworth became a friend of Van Buren's son, John, and an ally of the Radical or "Barnburner" faction of the state Democracy, along with Samuel J. Tilden, Silas Wright, John A. Dix and Sanford E. Church of Albion. They got their nickname because someone likened them to the farmer who burned down his barn to get rid of rats. Their conservative antagonists, led by William L. Marcy and Daniel S. Dickinson, were called "Hunkers," because they supposedly "hunkered" (hankered) after office.

During the years of national debate over slavery, Wadsworth stood with the anti-slavery forces on every issue. When he failed to make the Democratic party the vehicle of protest, he joined other camps.

The national campaign of 1848 saw him deserting the Democratic ticket headed by Lewis Cass, whom he called "a treacherous hybrid," for the Free Soilers, led by former

President Van Buren. The Van Burenites split the New York Democracy and threw the state and the Presidency to the Whig, Taylor.

As the storm clouds thickened, Wadsworth's dislike of human bondage and its arrogant Southern defenders mounted. He was an early convert to the new Republican party and worked for Fremont for President in 1856. He had strong support for the Republican gubernatorial nomination that year, but Thurlow Weed and William H. Seward, who had left the dying Whig party to boss the new one, put over John A. King through a coalition movement. Always a scrapper, Wadsworth fought to the last ditch.

The Genesee Valley squire was too independent to suit the old "dictator," Weed. Whenever Wadsworth aspired to office, the Weed-Seward machine blocked his path. In 1857 when he sought a seat in the Senate, Preston King got the bosses' nod.

Therefore it is not strange that the contest for the Republican presidential nomination in 1860 found Wadsworth lined up with the opponents of Seward, the favorite in the race. Wadsworth was not a delegate to the convention but he signed a letter which declared that Seward could not carry New York. That contention was not put to the test, for Abraham Lincoln, not the better known Seward, emerged with the prize.

After Lincoln's election there was some talk of a Cabinet post for Wadsworth but the selection of Seward to head the State Department ruled out any other New Yorker.

Lincoln welcomed Wadsworth at the White House and heard his appeal for giving state patronage to the anti-Sewardites. The new President said: "One side must not gobble up everything. Make a list of offices you want and I will endeavor to apply the rule of give and take." As it turned out, the Weed organization got more than its share of the spoils.

When it came to grabbing patronage plums, Horace Greeley and Wadsworth were outclassed by the old master, Weed.

Wadsworth was one of the 11 New York delegates to the futile Peace Congress in 1861. At the outbreak of hostilities, he led in forming a regiment in Livingston County which was called in his honor, the Wadsworth Guards. Officially it was the 104th Regiment of New York Volunteers.

As a civilian James Wadsworth proved his mettle in the early days of the war. When the land route to Washington was blocked through the destruction of bridges and railroad tracks North of Baltimore, he stocked a ferry boat in New York with supplies needed by the troops isolated at Annapolis. He recruited 100 workmen with tools and put them on the ship. Under his direction, his gang repaired the rail line and broke the blockade. The operation cost him some $17,000. Later he sent a boat load of Western New York cheese to the army.

He was 53 years old, white haired but erect and vigorous and he longed for active duty. He was awarded a major generalship by New York's Governor, Edwin D. Morgan, but resigned it when the Secretary of War ruled that commissions for general officers could be given out only by the federal government.

Still determined to get into service and although he was over the age limit for volunteers, he went to General McDowell, commanding the Union troops in Northern Virginia, and applied for duty as a staff aide. McDowell made him a major and the aristocratic land owner carried despatches and performed other lowly tasks as cheerfully as any "shavetail."

He got his baptism of fire and first heard the fearsome Rebel yell at Bull Run where he took part in the charge of the Eighth New York. He reformed the line after a repulse, but when the green troops ran into the gray-clad lines of

Thomas J. Jackson, "standing like a stone wall," they broke and ran, despite all of Wadsworth's efforts to rally them.

Major Wadsworth stayed at Fairfax Court House to see that none of the wounded, stragglers and worn out soldiers were left behind in the debacle. His conduct at Bull Run was commended by General McDowell.

In August, 1861, Wadsworth was commissioned a brigadier general in command of five New York regiments, stationed near Arlington, Va., and assigned to the defense of Washington. His second son, Craig, although only 20, was a member of his staff.

At Arlington and all through the war, General Wadsworth displayed rare concern for his men. He saw to it that they were well fed and decently housed. The tall, white-haired, chin-whiskered general would be seen at dawn poking around camp to see that the barracks were warm and ventilated. He stood for hours patiently teaching recruits how to build chimneys and fireplaces. He saw they had plenty of hot coffee. He was exacting about the care of the horses, for, like all Valley men, he knew horseflesh.

At his own expense he bought gloves for men on picket duty. He sent provisions to the needy in occupied territory as if they had been his own tenants. He cared for wandering slaves and his kindness sometimes paid off in information about the enemy gained from the Negroes. The general lived simply himself. It was said of him that he would never ask a soldier to do a thing he would not do himself. No wonder his troops were fond of the "Old Man."

In 1862 Wadsworth was made military governor of Washington, a highly responsible post, for there were constant fears of a Rebel raid on the capital. That began his feud with the egotistical commander of the Army of the Potomac, General George B. McClellan. "Little Mac" protested the appointment of an officer without engineering training, in charge of 25,000 men and the ring of fortifications around the capital. Lincoln, always sensitive to political situations, had named Wadsworth to conciliate Northern agricultural and Radical elements.

While he was military governor of Washington, Wadsworth set into motion the chain of events that McClellan partisans claimed prevented the Army of the Potomac from capturing Richmond.

Orders from McClellan taking four regiments from the defense of Washington sent a hotly protesting General Wadsworth to the office of War Secretary Stanton. He claimed his forces already were inadequate, as well as poorly trained. Egged on by Stanton and haunted by the fear of capture of his capital, Lincoln detached two divisions from McClellan's Peninsular campaign for the protection of Washington. McClellan charged that the President had broken his promise not to deplete the Army of the Potomac and thereby ruined his drive on Richmond.

Characteristically, Wadsworth saw to it that escaped Negroes were fed and sheltered when they sought refuge in Washington. He had many political prisoners, civilians seized on various charges, in his charge. He studied each case carefully.

Among those brought before him was a farmer named Patrick McCracken who lived near Fredericksburg, Va. and was accused of being a spy. Convinced that the man was not a dangerous security risk, the general released him on obtaining his pledge not to help the Rebel cause.

During his Washington assignment, Wadsworth was in close and frequent contact with Lincoln and became convinced that the President had no genuine feeling about slavery, sought merely to preserve the Union and acted upon military and political necessities.

In 1862 Horace Greeley and the Radicals, in control of the New York Republican convention, nominated General Wadsworth for governor on a "Win the War" platform. Lincoln's decision to issue the Emancipation Proclamation had swung the tide against the moderates under the old boss, Weed. The general's Democratic opponent was the popular former Governor, Horatio Seymour, an old hand at the political game, who condemned emancipation and the administration's conduct of the war.

Because of his military duties, Wadsworth declined to take the stump and made only one speech during the campaign, a ringing call in New York's Cooper Union for support of Lincoln and his war policies. Unlike Seymour, Wadsworth was not a polished orator but he radiated sincerity and earnestness on the platform.

A Union victory might have saved him but there were only Union reverses. So Seymour won by 10,000 votes. Wadsworth felt that the Weed-Seward forces had been less than vigorous in his behalf.

After the election, the general, at his request, was restored to active service with the Army of the Potomac. In December, 1862, he reported to General Burnside, in command of an army demoralized over the useless sacrifice of life and the humiliating defeat at Fredericksburg.

Wadsworth was given command of the First Division of the First Corps, which included the celebrated Iron Brigade of veteran Michigan and Wisconsin men of furious valor who wore black slouch hats as their emblem.

In Winter quarters, after he saw that the sharp-hoofed mules sank in the mire, he used logs for foundations of roads and his men called him "Old Corduroy." He procured oxen to replace the mules and showed his men how to handle the beasts.

Then came Chancellorsville and Gettysburg and the high tide of the war. On the march to Gettysburg, Wadsworth had shoes taken from the feet of civilians and distributed among his soldiers. On the first day of Gettysburg, his division bore the brunt of the first gray wave and, outnumbered, had to fall back. Later they rallied and shared in the glory of that far from complete victory.

After Gettysburg, the general went on detached service, investigating the condition of Negro troops and civilians in the conquered Mississippi Valley. He offered a plan for organizing freedmen into self-sustaining farm colonies. He also served on a military court of inquiry early in 1864 and as a commissioner in charge of the exchange of prisoners.

When he learned that the dogged Grant had been given supreme command of the Union legions, he obtained an assignment to the Army of the Potomac, for he knew there would be action with Grant at the helm. Wadsworth was given a division and he improved the morale of his troops by getting them comfortable quarters and new shoes. He insisted that the shoes, as well as the brass and guns, be kept polished.

Grant decided to march through the Wilderness, hoping to avoid a battle in that wooded jungle. But smack in the center of the forest, the two armies clashed. Lee had 61,000 men to Grant's 115,000 but the Rebels were familiar with that dark and treacherous terrain.

Wadsworth plunged his division into the tangle where his men stumbled and were blinded by smoke. They ran into a remorseless enemy fire and were outflanked. The woods were on fire and trapped men screamed in pain. There was no line of battle and the slaughter was terrible that day when two great armies collided in the thick forest.

On the second day Wadsworth, waving the saber an ancestor had carried in the Revolution, rode up and down his lines, regrouping his shattered command. The tall, white-haired warrior was tired and sick, and he considered turning over his command to someone else, but decided to stick it out.

Again, despite his shouts of "Give it to 'em, Bucktails," as he rode at the head of the column, his division was pushed back. Two horses were shot from under Wadsworth that day and finally a Rebel bullet caught him in the head. Of the 5,000 he had marched into the Wilderness, only 500 were left —and he was mortally wounded.

An officer of Lee's staff found the general with a piece of paper pinned to his blue coat for identification, his left hand grasping the stock of a musket on the ground. He was taken to a field hospital behind the lines.

There on the evening of May 7, 1864, a man came and said: "My name is Patrick McCracken and I have a little farm hereabouts. I have heard General Wadsworth is wounded and I want to do something for him."

It was the same McCracken Wadsworth had released from prison in Washington in 1862. The farmer brought fresh milk to the dying man and said he would return.

When next he came, the general was dead. McCracken got permission to bury the body on his land and wrote the general's widow a simple account of her husband's passing. A Wadsworth son-in-law, Montgomery Ritchie, a few weeks later went to Fredericksburg, where the remains had been taken under a flag of truce. Then the general went home to the Valley for the last time.

Geneseo was draped in mourning the day of the military

funeral. The general sleeps under the elms in the family plot in Temple Hill Cemetery. His tombstone is a massive granite block, ornamented with flag-draped urn, cannon, sword, epaulets and laurel wreath, along with the names of the battles in which he fought.

James S. Wadsworth was an amateur general, as were so many others in the Civil War. He may not have been the outstanding military tactician of the conflict, but he stands head and shoulders above the most of the so-called "political generals." He was brave as a lion and he looked after his men. He was a patrician and a politician—who also was a patriot.

Chapter 14

Telegraph Titans

The date is May 24, 1844. The scene is the chamber of the United States Supreme Court in Washington.

Judges, Congressmen, the elite of officialdom watch as the graceful fingers that had won Samuel Finley Breese Morse acclaim as a painter tap out on the key of an instrument he had invented four words:

"What hath God wrought!"

Over the 40 miles of wires stretching from the Capitol to the Baltimore & Ohio Railway station in Baltimore flashes the first message ever sent by magnetic telegraph.

The Very Important People shower congratulations on the inventor. Not many weeks before some of them had opposed the paltry $30,000 appropriation he had wangled from Congress to build the pioneer test line.

None of those present sensed the tremendous import of that moment in history. They could not know that the Morse gadget was the forerunner of the oceanic cables, the telephone, the radio, radar, television and all the electronic wonders of today.

At the other end of the line, in the Pratt Street depot in Baltimore, the solemn visage of a tall, rawboned man with a wispy chinwhisker broke into a rare, quick smile. The Lincolnesque figure was named Ezra Cornell.

He had had no small share in that day's triumph. For he had bossed the construction of the line. When his employers wanted him to dig a ditch in which to lay the lead pipe that was to carry the wires, he had devised a trenching machine. After he and Morse agreed that wires strung on wooden poles would be more practicable, he had solved the problem of insulation by using a simple glass knob which could be safely attached to the poles.

In his 37 years Ezra Cornell had worked hard at many things but none of them had turned out very well.

When he was a babe, his Quaker parents had brought him from his birthplace in Columbia County to the frontier settlement of De Ruyter in the County of Madison. He got a little schooling in the Winters and was good at ciphering, but most of the time he had to work on his father's farm and in his pottery.

Young Ezra was forever tinkering and building things. He was only 17 when, without help, he built a stout frame house for his family. Two years later the gangling six-footer left home to work as an itinerant carpenter. He did some lumbering along the Erie Canal, then worked in a machine shop at Homer.

One day in 1828, with all his possessions in a bag slung over his shoulder, he tramped the 20 odd miles from Homer to Ithaca. It was his first visit to the picturesque town at the head of Cayuga Lake and it was a case of love at first sight. Ezra Cornell was to live there the rest of his days.

He obtained worked as a millwright and was given the job of overhauling mills along Fall Creek. He simplified the milling operations by blasting and boring a tunnel 200 feet through the rocky gorge. That tunnel is still in use.

He lost his job in the panic of 1839 and tried his hand at farming. By then he was a husband and the father of a seven-year-old boy who was named Alonzo and was to become a governor of New York. Ezra's marriage out of the Quaker faith brought his excommunication from the Society of Friends. Mary Ann meant more to him than his religion. And he was more than a little stubborn.

Ithaca fell into the economic doldrums after the collapse of a boom built on a canal from Sodus Bay to Cayuga Lake that never was dug. Business men of the village sent Cornell to Eastern cities in a campaign to "sell" Ithaca as a manufacturing site. But the big town capitalists remained unsold after they noted the village's isolated inland location on the map.

Cornell's next endeavor, selling a plow that had been patented by two Ithaca neighbors, carried him from Maine to Georgia. In Portland, Maine, he made the acquaintance of F. O. J. Smith, a publisher who was one of the original Morse patentees. Smith had the contract to build the first telegraph line and he engaged Cornell to boss the job.

So it was that the lean Ithacan was on hand at the birth of the telegraph industry. He had boundless faith in it. The federal government would not subsidize or operate it, so it had to be developed by private enterprise.

Cornell was employed by Smith to demonstrate the telegraph in Boston and New York. He came to be regarded as the outstanding technical expert on the subject. Former Postmaster General Amos Kendall came into the field as manager for the bulk of the Morse interests and proposed a network of trunk lines linking the nation's major cities. For that purpose the Magnetic Telegraph Company, first in the United States, was organized. Cornell was named its construction chief and he put $500 of his meager hoard into the enterprise. The new company's first line ran from New York to Philadelphia.

By 1845 "telegraph fever" was sweeping the country and there were four rival companies in the field, all using the Morse patent and all turning to Cornell, the expert, for counsel.

There ensued a titanic struggle for control of the industry that raged for more than a decade. In it three Upstate figures stand out. They were Ezra Cornell of Ithaca, Henry O'Reilly of Albany and Hiram Sibley of Rochester, a latecomer in the arena but the greatest gladiator of them all.

O'Reilly had been an early editor and Jacksonian leader in Rochester and had written the first history of the Flour City in 1838. He was a fiery, romantic, convivial, rosy-cheeked Irishman to whom the telegraph battle was a crusade.

Backed largely by Rochester money, he formed the Atlantic, Lake and Mississippi Valley Telegraph Company with the idea of controlling all the lines West of Philadelphia. He began with a line from Lancaster to Harrisburg over the protests of the Pennsylvania Dutch farmers who considered the telegraph an instrument of the devil.

O'Reilly, an exponent of the frontal attack, believed that the company that built the most lines would win the war. He built too many lines in too many directions in too short a time. Court actions helped to unhorse him, but it was over-expansion that ruined the likeable Irishman in the end.

In the meantime Cornell had risen out of the employe class. He invested all he had and all he could raise to gain control of several short lines in Michigan and Canada. He triumphed over the tottering O'Reilly in the West. He promoted a line along the route of the new Erie Railroad from the Hudson to Lake Erie and before it was completed, had to borrow money to replace his threadbare clothes.

For many trying months the swarthy, taciturn former mechanic rode across many states on slow trains and stages, doing with little sleep, stopping to direct the repair of his lines, maneuvering, dickering in the ceaseless chess game of the wires.

At last things seemed to be going his way. His own little telegraph empire appeared impregnable. True there was a small cloud in the sky above Rochester but Cornell discounted its importance.

Judge Samuel L. Selden and Freeman Edson had the exclusive rights to the House printing machine, a complicated rival of the simple Morse instrument and were operating a line from New York to Buffalo, the New York State Telegraph Printing Company. They began to look Westward for new fields.

They interested a successful business man of Rochester named Hiram Sibley in their enterprise. Strong featured, forceful, smooth shaven in a time when men were bearded, he was a blend of boldness, determination, vision and Yankee shrewdness.

As a sturdy youth of 16, Sibley had come to the Genesee Country with his family in 1823 from his birthplace, North Adams, Mass. Like Ezra Cornell he had a lot of mechanical know how. Before he was 21 he had mastered five trades. He learned the cobbler's trade in his teens.

He worked in mills around Lima and Honeoye Falls and spent his first winter in Western New York repairing the wheels and gears in the woolen mills at Factory Hollow. He learned the wool carder and cotton spinner trades in mills at Mount Morris and Sparta. His father had set up a saw mill in the Town of Mendon and the settlement that grew up around it was named Sibleyville. Then Hiram Sibley went into partnership with Don Alonzo Watson in operating a machine shop-foundry at Sibleyville that made carding machines and farm implements. In 1830 it employed 30 hands.

In 1843, when he was elected sheriff of Monroe County as a Van Buren Free Soil Democrat from Mendon, Sibley had his only fling at politics. After his term ended, he made his home in Rochester, where he entered the real estate field.

He quickly assumed command of the Rochester telegraph group. He put every dollar he owned and many borrowed ones into the enterprise. When because of lack of funds, the projected line to St. Louis had only reached Louisville, Sibley announced a bold plan. He put his finger on the elemental weakness of the industry. There were 40 competing lines, only two or three of them really profitable. Local rivalries, duplicating costs, patent litigation, inefficient management throttled the chaotic young industry.

Sibley proposed that the short, unprofitable lines west of Buffalo be merged into one giant company. At a meeting of the Rochester group in 1854, he asked each of the 25 men present to subscribe $5,000 to carry out his scheme. A few refused—to their lasting regret. When finally $90,000 was pledged, the Sibley-led forces embarked on a career of conquest seldom duplicated in corporate history.

Gripsack in hand, the vigorous Sibley went up and down the land, picking up at bargain prices the stock of the weaker companies until he had control. He gobbled up the Morse lines in the West, one by one. He squeezed Cornell by stealthy raids until the Ithaca man, tired and ailing, acting on the axiom, "If you can't beat 'em, jine 'em," threw in the sponge and joined the merger in 1855.

On April 4, 1856, the Western Union Telegraph Company, a name for the combination which was suggested by Cornell, was organized in Room 22, the office of Don Alonzo Watson, Sibley's old partner, in Rochester's old Reynolds Arcade. Hiram Sibley was chosen its president, an office he held for 20 eventful years.

There were anxious days when Western Union's payroll was barely met. The timorous sold out and Sibley bought their stock. He kept raiding rival companies. He never rested.

In 1858 he urged the directors to build a line 2,000 miles long from St. Louis to the Pacific Coast. The boldness of the idea scared the directors and they turned it down. Then Hiram Sibley squared his shoulders, thrust out his chin and rose from the table, announcing:

"Gentlemen, if you will not join me, I will go it alone."

Go it alone he did. In 1861 he made a contract with the government in his own name to construct the line in two years under a federal subsidy which was to be paid off in 10 years.

In the stupendous task of stringing the wires across treeless plains and great mountains, Sibley proved himself a masterly diplomat as well as builder. He pacified hostile Indians who threatened to rip the poles from their ancient buffalo hunting grounds. He tapped a wire on the plains and told a listening Sioux chieftain that the clicking he heard was "the Voice of the Great Spirit." The Indian was overcome with awe. There was no trouble with the Redskins. One chief sent Sibley a black tailed buck deer which eventually died of old age in Rochester.

After the Civil War broke out, sabotage by border ruffians in Missouri forced the bypassing of that state for Iowa and Nebraska. The obstacles were tremendous. Wires and insulators had to be shipped from New York to San Francisco via Cape Horn and hauled miles inland. More than 1,000 oxen were used in the job. Many of the poles came from Brigham Young's Mormons in Salt Lake City.

On Oct. 24, 1861, the oceans were linked by the wires. Sibley had completed the Western project in four months, instead of the stipulated two years. Western Union formed a subsidiary, Pacific Telegraph, and took the line over. It proved valuable to the Union during the war.

It was the turning point in the fortunes of the company. In 1863 Western Union stock soared to 225 and paid a 100 per cent. dividend. Rochesterians were mortgaging their homes, selling their carriage horses, borrowing money to buy Western Union stock. It formed the basis of some considerable fortunes.

The Civil War boomed Western Union but it ruined its principal rival, American Telegraph, whose lines stretched across the battle zones. Soon Western Union gobbled up American, after absorbing the upstart United States Telegraph Company. Then the Rochester-born colossus emerged as the absolute ruler of the wire kingdom, a forty million dollar corporation, largest in the nation and America's first giant monopoly.

A pet Sibley scheme was linking the United States with Europe by a telegraph line across Alaska, then a Russian possession; the Bering Strait and Siberia. After hundreds of miles of lines had been built and three millions spent on the overland project, it had to be abandoned. It was killed by Cyrus Field's final success in laying the Atlantic Cable in 1866.

But the line that never was completed led to the purchase of Alaska from Russia by the United States—thanks largely to Hiram Sibley. In 1865 the Western Union president was in St. Petersburg to confer with the Russian Prime Minister on the international line. Sibley learned through his talks with the premier that Russia would sell Alaska for a reasonable sum. Immediately he transmitted the news to the State Department and two years later Secretary Seward negotiated the purchase of what will be the 49th state of the Union.

In 1866 Sibley retired as president of Western Union and that year the company shifted its headquarters from Rochester, its birthplace, to New York City. Sibley retained large holdings in the corporation he had fathered and was a very rich man. But he was not one to sit still.

He plunged into promotion and management of railroads in the Mid West and South; he developed a lumber and salt business at Saginaw, Mich.; he farmed 40,000 acres in Illinois and in the late 1870s was considered the largest farm owner in the country.

He traveled widely and brought many rare paintings back from Europe to his big house on Rochester's East Avenue. Another hobby was his vegetable garden and he proudly showed the enormous tomatoes he raised.

As his fortune piled up, he turned to philanthropy and became interested in the University of Rochester. He contemplated giving an engineering school to the local college but found its president, Dr. Martin B. Anderson, an old line Baptist clergyman, lukewarm toward scientific education.

But when Dr. Anderson fought Ezra Cornell's proposed land grant university at Cornell because it was "non sectarian," an aroused Hiram Sibley sprang to the defense of his former associate. He announced the gift to Cornell of the $200,000 Sibley School of Mechanical Arts and was made a trustee of the University.

Backers of the Rochester university, alarmed at the turn of events, hastened to mollify the local magnate. They made him a trustee of the U. of R. and in 1877 he gave $100,000 for the erection of Sibley Hall, a library-museum.

Sibley and Anderson differed politely about the form of the gift. Sibley wanted a museum to house the rare collections of the eminent Rochester naturalist, Henry A. Ward. The college president wanted a library. So the compromise

196

came about. In his lifetime Sibley made later substantial gifts to the University and remembered the college liberally in his will.

The seed house of Hiram Sibley & Co. was founded in Rochester in the 1870s and it became one of the most important in the trade. A nine-story building was erected on upper East Main Street and in the early 1880s the company was employing 500, many of them traveling agents and managers of experimental seed farms scattered over the land. Hiram Sibley never did anything on a small scale.

Death came to the founder of an empire of wires in 1888. He was 81. After him his son, Hiram W., carried on the far flung family interests. Now the head of the numerous clan is a grandson, Harper Sibley, onetime president of the United States Chamber of Commerce, who lives, as the family always has, on Rochester's East Avenue and is an internationally known churchman. He has a particular affection for one of the least of his holdings, a few acres in Sibleyville—where in the 1820s the young master of five trades started a little machine shop.

*   *   *

Whatever resentment Ezra Cornell may have felt when he was forced to yield his telegraph holdings evaporated when the golden flood of Western Union profits came rolling in. His Erie & Michigan stock valued at $50,000 in 1857 was worth two million dollars in 1865.

He was at heart a farmer and had bought 300 acres on lordly East Hill above Ithaca and Cayuga's waters, along with two smaller farms. He lived in a rambling farmhouse, called his place Forest Park and kept busy setting out fruit trees, buying live stock and promoting agricultural societies. In

1862 he was named president of the State Agricultural Society.

Elected to the Assembly as a Republican in 1861, Cornell's first official act was to return the pass the Erie Railroad had presented him.

In 1863, a banner year for Western Union, Cornell discovered "he had more money than he or his family would need" and the philanthropic phase of his career began. He bought a lot in downtown Ithaca and on it erected at his own expense the Cornell Free Library, which is still serving the public.

As head of the State Agricultural Society, he was an *ex officio* trustee of the little State Agricultural College at Ovid on Seneca Lake, which, despite its name, was financed by farming interests without state aid. It had to close its doors in 1861 when the Civil War drained off its students and faculty.

After passage of the Morrill Act under which each state received a share of the public lands for the endowment of a college, Cornell and other Ovid trustees in 1863 petitioned for the grant. So did Senator Charles Cook in behalf of the People's College he had fathered in his home town of Havana (now Montour Falls). Cook won the grant on condition his college raise $242,000. When it failed to do so, Cornell, by then elevated to the State Senate, proposed dividing the grant between the Ovid and Havana schools.

In the Senate he met cultured Andrew D. White, representing the Syracuse district. White had his own ideas about the state university. He urged Cornell to establish a brand new college with his own fortune and the land grant funds.

At a meeting of the trustees of the defunct Ovid College in 1864, Ezra Cornell rose and read from a slip of paper. The message electrified the gathering. He proposed that if the state land grant college be located at Ithaca, he would give his 300 acre farm, erect on it suitable buildings and endow the new college with $300,000.

In the Legislature the bill embodying his offer met strong opposition, particularly from denominational leaders such as Anderson of Rochester. The legislation finally passed, largely because of Cornell's $300,000 pledge. Cook of Havana could not match that. Nor could anyone else. It was Western Union profits that made Cornell University possible.

On Oct. 8, 1868, "the freshwater college" on the hill opened with 388 students when only half that number had been expected. Only one building was completed. So Cascadilla Place, a former water cure owned by Cornell, was put into service and jammed with students and teachers.

Out of that beginning grew the present great "Ivy League" university on Ezra Cornell's old hilltop farm "far above Cayuga's waters."

The ideals of the university are stated in these words of its founder, emblazoned on its shield:

"I would found an institution where any person can find instruction in any study."

Financial worries clouded Cornell's last years. He lost money on a pet plan to make Ithaca the hub of a network of small railroads. Always his heart was set on making Ithaca a big city. It remained a smallish city but a most attractive and distinctive one.

Cornell mortgaged his personal property when his fortunes skidded. He managed the affairs of the university better than he did his own. His able handling of the public lands it received from the government kept his college on a firm financial footing and assured it a steady income during early, parlous years.

The lean old man with the stringy chinwhisker whose

199

stony facade hid the fires that burned within him, the mechanic who had built the first telegraph line in America, died on Dec. 9, 1874 in his Ithaca home.

It has been well said of Ezra Cornell that "He built for all time."

Chapter 15

Richmond of the Rails

Dean Richmond was a six foot giant with a roaring voice and features as rough hewn as his native Vermont. In keeping with his physical stature, he did everything on the grand scale, whether he was manipulating a board of directors, bossing a political convention or building the biggest, most elegant mansion in Batavia with silver fittings in its bathroom.

Yankee-shrewd, iron-willed, resourceful, farsighted, he was often brusque but beneath the bluster was a warm-hearted, outgiving, generous nature.

An accomplished poker player who delighted in high stakes, he rose from poverty to the presidency of the New York Central Railroad and the leadership of the Democratic party in New York State through his own efforts and with little formal education.

Born in Woodstock, Vt., in 1804, he was a small child when his family moved to Salina, now a part of Syracuse, where his father entered the booming salt industry. The senior Richmond came a financial cropper and died when Dean was 15. The support of his widowed mother and two sisters fell to the hulking lad.

He got a job in a store, saved his pay and went into the salt business on his own. He succeeded where his father had failed. There's a story—and the legends cluster about this colorful figure—that he helped a widow settle an estate with such skill that she lent him $4,000, which he put into railroad stocks, his first of many investments in that industry.

As a boy he had watched the digging of the Erie Canal and when it was done, marveled at the mighty stream of traffic on the lazy waters and at the towns that sprang up on its banks.

Then in the 1830s the first clumsy wood-burning locomotives began dragging the cars over crude iron rails. The era of the Iron Horse had dawned. Short competing lines within a few years linked Upstate towns—the Mohawk & Hudson, the Utica & Schenectady, the Tonawanda from Rochester to Batavia and eventually Attica; the Syracuse & Utica, the Attica & Buffalo, the Syracuse & Auburn, the Rochester & Auburn.

Young Richmond decided the railroad was the coming thing. He saw it would forge a firm link with the burgeoning West. In 1842 he moved to the booming lake port of Buffalo, gateway to the West. There he entered the shipping business on the Great Lakes. He built the Richmond Elevator at the old Buffalo Dock. He made a lot of money fast. He became a director of the Rochester & Buffalo Railway, successor to the pioneer Tonawanda road. Later he was made president of the Buffalo & State Line, which ran along Lake Erie. And in due time he was elected a bank director in Buffalo.

After three years spent in Syracuse looking after his interests there, he moved in 1848 to Attica, then a brisk railroad center. In 1852 he established residence in Batavia and built his mansion on the village's principal street. He developed a strong affection for the town and when he was boss of the New York Central, he insisted that all trains stop there.

But as long as he lived, Buffalo remained the headquarters

of his business enterprises. Two days of each week he spent in the quiet of his Batavia home.

His mansion, an imposing relic of an expansive era, now is the Batavia Children's Home. Dean Richmond spared no expense when he built the great gray brick house with four massive Ionic pillars, surrounded by grounds and gardens. In its day it was the showplace of the region. There were thick yellow velvet carpets on the floors, yellow damask tapestry on the walls, mirrors that reached from floor to ceiling, besides the before mentioned silver trimmings in the bath room. Lavish balls and parties were held in the mansion. Dean Richmond's manners were homespun but his way of life was ostentatious.

By 1850 the canal packet was no more and the stage coaches were outmoded. The railroad was the thing. But railroad leaders looked askance at the chain of 12 competing lines stretched across the state from Albany to Buffalo and saw how consolidation would save money, end duplications and benefit service. It was a state legislative committee that first proposed the move in 1851. Two years later consolidation received state sanction and the 12 lines were merged into the New York Central Railroad system.

Richmond, as president of one road and a director of another, was a leader in the merger and was made a director and vice president, second in command of the system.

Chosen president was Erastus Corning, Albany Democrat, founder of a political dynasty in the capital city, an iron maker and a cripple with autocratic ways. For 12 years he had headed the Utica & Schenectady without pay. However, his factories had furnished the rails and most of the equipment for the road, and he was a very rich man.

Richmond, a life-long Democrat allied to the old Van Buren wing of the party, grew in political influence and looked after the New York Central's interests at the state capitol. He did not hesitate to work with Republicans when it was necessary. He had Thurlow Weed, the state Republican boss, in his corner pushing legislation helpful to the Central and killing bills that were not. Richmond also got Weed's political partner, William H. Seward, on the railroad's payroll as a counsel.

There was stiff competition among the railroads in the 1850s and 1860s. The Central waged a long rate war with the New York and Erie, which in 1851 had completed its line across Southern New York from the Hudson to Dunkirk on Lake Erie. And in New York City a powerful figure was rising in the realm of the rails. Cornelius Vanderbilt, the fabulous old Commodore, controlled the New York & Harlem and New York and Hudson River lines operating Northward from the metropolis.

The year 1864 saw a fierce battle within the Central for control of the system. Two slates were entered in the election. On the ticket which sought the ouster of President Corning was Hiram Sibley, the Rochester telegraph magnate. Dean Richmond was on both slates. The Corning forces scored a smashing victory. Then Erastus Corning, who had sought vindication, resigned his post. He was 70, ill and tired. Richmond was chosen as his successor. No one else was considered for the presidency of the New York Central.

The new president was bolder and possessed greater vision than his predecessor. Richmond made a truce with the Vanderbilts after he had turned down the Commodore's proposal that the Central lease the two down-river lines. Richmond pushed to completion a long and expensive bridge over the Hudson between Albany and Troy in 1866 and he got the Vanderbilt road, the New York & Hudson River, to use the span and the Central's terminal in Albany. The Boston & Albany also used the bridge and the terminal.

During Richmond's reign, he doubletracked the Central system. He was a pioneer advocate of the use of steel rails, instead of iron. He had ordered a large quantity from England and had supervised a test of them on the Central just before his death in 1866.

In the meantime he had achieved national political stature. He worked with New York millionaires August Belmont and Samuel J. Tilden, in building a state Democratic machine. In 1860 Richmond was chairman of the Democratic state committee and led the Empire State delegation to the ill-fated national convention in Charleston.

There he strove with Belmont and others to keep the Southern delegates from bolting when they balked at nominating Stephen A. Douglas. Richmond advanced Horatio Seymour of New York as a compromise candidate. He offered the Dixie bloc important concessions in the writing of the platform. But all his work was in vain. Most of the Southern delegates took a walk.

At the second convention in Baltimore two months later Richmond again offered Seymour and tried to heal the sectional rift. But the Douglas forces kept to their "rule or ruin" policy and Virginia led a new bolt from the convention hall.

So the South named its own candidates, the Democratic vote was divided and the Republican, Abraham Lincoln, coasted to victory. Then came secession and Civil War—which Dean Richmond had striven to avert.

During the war years Richmond kept his state chairmanship and control of the party machine. He persuaded Seymour to run for Governor in 1862 and forced him on the state convention. Seymour won and Richmond supported the Governor in his vigorous opposition to the workings of the draft and other administration policies.

In 1864 Richmond headed the New York delegation to the Democratic national convention that nominated General McClellan for the Presidency. This time he stifled a demand among delegates for Seymour.

After the war he supported President Johnson in his struggle with the Radical Republicans. Richmond had no particular love for Andy Johnson but he saw a chance to divide the Republicans. With the deposed Republican boss, Weed, and the rising Democrat, Tilden, he became a leader in the National Union party which rallied behind Johnson and opposed harsh measures in dealing with the beaten South.

Richmond managed the state convention of the conservative Republican-Democratic coalition at Saratoga in 1866 and caught a severe cold at the meeting. But when a week later he left Batavia for the national convention of the splinter party at Philadelphia, he seemed to have recovered. In the midst of the session he was stricken gravely ill. His political comrades, Tilden and Judge Sanford E. Church of Albion, took him to the New York residence of Tilden where he died on Aug. 18, 1866.

He was only 62 years old. Doctors said he had overtaxed his strength.

The locomotive and the coaches of the special train that took him back to Batavia were draped in black, as were all the shops, engines and cars of the Central lines. His funeral was the biggest in Batavia's history. St. James Episcopal Church, which had often been the recipient of his bounty, was crowded. Among those who attended were former President Fillmore, Tilden, Seymour, Weed and a host of other political and financial potentates. After the service, hundreds of mourners, marching four abreast, followed the hearse, drawn by six horses, to the old Batavia Cemetery. There close to the Central tracks, Dean Richmond sleeps in a family mausoleum as big as a house.

Richmond died at the zenith of his political and financial power. After his death the National Union movement fell apart and Tammany gobbled up the state Democracy. New hands grasped the throttle of the New York Central and they were no match for Cornelius Vanderbilt. Within a few months the old Commodore had taken over the system.

Had Richmond lived the story might have been different. Had the Upstater elected to fight it out with Vanderbilt, the battle of those two giants would have been epic. Again Richmond might have made some shrewd compromise. He was an artful poker player.

In Western New York they still repeat the stories that grew up around the rugged extrovert who was Batavia's first citizen. They say his handwriting was so execrable that once after he had fired an employe in writing, that worthy for years used the letter with the unmistakable signature at the end and the rest illegible, as a pass on the Central.

And there's the tale about the sycophantic bore who haunted Richmond's office, begging for a pass on the railroad. Finally the big man with the roaring voice wrote out a pass. It was for only one way—and for a faraway place.

All over Batavia you run across the name, Richmond, although none of the family now live in the old shire town of Genesee County. There's the stone Richmond Memorial Public Library, given by the magnate's widow in memory of a son, Dean, Jr.; the once elegant Richmond Hotel, no longer elegant; Richmond Avenue and the big house that is now a Children's Home.

Chapter 16

Two for the Money

Wells, Fargo—what a romantic picture of the Old West those two names conjure up.

Red wheels roll along the trails behind six horses, bearing the miners' nuggets and dust to the Coast Towns in the Gold Rush of the 1850s . . . Messengers with shot guns perch beside the drivers, ready to defend their rich cargoes at the risk of their lives, and many of them die . . . Fierce storms rake the desert and the mountains but somehow the red wagons of Wells, Fargo—and in Winter the red sleighs—get through . . . The picturesque Pony Express, riders dashing half way across a continent with the mails and the express—that, too, was Wells, Fargo before telegraph lines and the Iron Horse came.

In that rich saga, the Wells, Fargo of song and story, the two Upstate New Yorkers who had started it all, Henry Wells and William George Fargo, played only absentee-owner roles.

Wells and Fargo were two-fisted men, far from colorless, but during those glamorous years of the express line that bore their names, they were far from the Western front. Wells did make one trip to the Coast but otherwise they were busy back East in their offices, running a veritable express empire and watching the dollars pile up.

In 1852, when they met in the backroom of a store in

Syracuse to hatch Wells, Fargo & Co., in a determined move to grab the Gold Rush business on the Pacific Coast from Alvin Adams, Henry Wells was 47 years old. Fargo was 13 years his junior. They had climbed far but the ascent had not been easy.

Wells was a chubby six footer with a massive Roman nose and a brown beard. In later years when his hair and whiskers whitened, he resembled Santa Claus. He was a merry soul and prankish. "Stuttering" Wells they called him before he became an express magnate. He spent a lot of money trying to cure his stammering but to the end he would stutter in times of stress. After he became affluent he set up schools for stammerers all over the country.

He was born in Vermont in 1805, the son of a Presbyterian pastor, who moved his family to New York State when the boy was very young. After serving churches in Fayette and Seneca Falls, the senior Wells came to Palmyra in 1814. He preached for two years in that village, then turned to farming.

When Henry was 16, he was apprenticed to Jessup & Palmer, Palmyra tanners. Deacon Jessup wanted all of his apprentices to attend his church and to sit together in the gallery. When Henry protested he had no suitable clothes, the deacon fitted him out with some of his own castoffs. The next Sunday Henry went to church, but instead of going into the gallery, he strode grandly down the aisle and seated himself in the Jessup pew, to the deacon's vast chagrin.

Before he was 20 he took a bride, Sarah (Dolly) Daggett, who lived in a little old house on Palmyra's Main Street that was torn down not so long ago. The dwelling was so small and the guests so many that the preacher married Henry and Sarah in its doorway before a yard full of spectators. Sarah died in 1859 and Wells remarried in 1861.

209

After the opening of the Erie Canal, Wells worked as a shoemaker in a shop near the Ditch in Port Byron for three years. He went to New York and got a job as runner for boats at the docks there. He struck up a valuable friendship with the crafty, eccentric stock market operator, "Uncle Dan'l" Drew, owner of the Hudson River steamboats. Wells became a forwarder and shipper on the Drew boats, on the Erie Canal, the Great Lakes and the Pennsylvania Railroad. He made friends easily and liked the shipping business.

His experience in handling parcels won him the job of Albany agent for William Harnden's pioneer express line which ran from Albany to Boston. Wells at once proposed extending the line to Buffalo and even predicted one day there would be an express line to the Pacific Coast. He was laughed at.

In 1841 he joined the express company of Pomeroy & Livingston as manager and shipping agent for a line from Albany to Buffalo, the route he had advocated two years earlier.

His title was pretentious but actually he was only a messenger. Early risers in Albany one morning might have seen a tall, ruddy, bearded man, wearing a greatcoat and a beaver hat and carrying a carpet bag, hurrying to the railroad station. That was Henry Wells on his maiden trip and in the carpetbag were cash and commercial paper.

The trip was an arduous one, by train from Albany to Auburn, then by stage to Geneva, by train to Rochester and on by rail to Batavia and Buffalo. The whole trip took two days. When Buffalo dealers clamored for fresh oysters, Wells added merchandise to his cargo.

This one-man express line also carried mail and incurred the wrath of Uncle Sam by cutting to six cents the government letter rate of 25 cents from New York to Buffalo.

Wells's company provided its own orange colored stamps. The government lost its suit to prevent the rate cutting. The rate war ended in 1845 when the legal letter rate was fixed by the government at five cents. There's a story that during the stamp feud the rural toll takers would lower their gates on the government carriers and let the jovial Wells through.

Wells became a partner in the Pomeroy-Livingston enterprise and in 1843 induced an acquaintance, William G. Fargo, to leave his job as freight agent at Auburn for the new Syracuse & Auburn Railroad and join him in the express business.

Fargo was a hard headed, energetic business man, less loquacious and shorter of stature than Wells, but just as amiable. He developed a taste for ostentatious living but his early years were rugged ones.

He was born in Pompey in Onondaga County, the same hilltop village that produced Leonard Jerome, the publisher-plunger-playboy grandfather of Winston Churchill, and Horatio Seymour, once Democratic candidate for the Presidency.

William Fargo was a son of a veteran of the War of 1812 and one of 12 children. At the age of 13 he was carrying the mail on horseback on a 30 mile circuit around Pompey. After working in a grocery in Weedsport, his only deviation from the transport business, he took the freight agent post at Auburn where Wells found him. After working for a time as a messenger, Fargo became local agent at Buffalo for the Pomeroy people.

In 1844, before a rail had been laid West of Buffalo, Wells and Fargo founded an express line from Buffalo to Detroit, Cincinnati, Chicago and St. Louis. They operated by stage, steamer and wagon train. This became the Western Express under Fargo's direction while Wells ran the New York to Buffalo line under the name of Wells & Co.

Wells, Fargo and five other leaders of the industry met in the Mansion House in Buffalo one day in 1852 and joined their forces in the American Express Co. with Henry Wells as president and William Fargo as secretary. This combination had virtual control of the business in the East and Mid West.

But in California, where gold had been struck, Alvin Adams was reaping a rich harvest carrying the miners' gold from the interior to the Coastal cities. Wells, Fargo and their associates determined to invade this promising new field.

So in 1852 the firm of Wells, Fargo & Co. was conceived, with ample capital, to operate an express between New York and San Francisco by boat, except for the overland passage of the Isthmus of Panama, and to operate interior lines on the new "Gold Coast." Edwin B. Morgan of Aurora on Cayuga Lake, where Wells had built a stately stone house, was chosen president of the new outfit but its real powers were Wells and Fargo.

It was not long before the new company, with its superior resources, had conquered the Adams Express on the Coast and was flourishing like the green bay tree. By 1860 Wells, Fargo had a virtual monopoly of the business in the Far West and the partners were wealthy men. Wells, Fargo absorbed a veritable staging empire in the West, including the Pony Express which operated 2,000 miles from St. Joseph, Mo., to San Francisco in nine days on a regular schedule. When the telegraph wires were strung and the rails laid across the Western half of the continent, the romantic Pony Express gave up the ghost.

Wells was ailing and tired and when the American Express Company was reorganized in 1868, he retired and Fargo succeeded him as president. Fargo had been the active director of the business and Wells had governed fiscal matters in late years.

Wells now had the time—and the means—to consummate a project dear to his heart, the founding of a women's college at Aurora. After he had held many conferences with two other philanthropists, Matthew Vassar and Ezra Cornell, the doors of his Wells Seminary for the Higher Education of Young Women opened in 1868. He gave the college its first building and an 111-acre campus. In 1870 the name of the school was shortened to Wells College.

Henry Wells died in 1878 in Glasgow, Scotland, during one of his frequent European tours. Business reverses in his last years prevented him from making the princely endowment to Wells College that he had planned.

Wells College today is much as Henry Wells planned it —a smallish non sectarian liberal arts college with rich traditions and high standards. Wells's old home, Glen Park, is part of the campus which stretches down the hillside to the blue Cayuga waters. The college girls are proud of a genuine Wells, Fargo stage coach that saw service in the West. It is trotted out on all gala days.

W. G. Fargo never retired. He remained in the express harness as long as he lived. This energetic, venturesome man with the wide eyes and the shaggy brown beard was the expansive type. After the death of Dean Richmond, president of the New York Central, Fargo and Henry Keep got control of the railroad system but they could not hold it against the onslaught of the tough old Commodore Vanderbilt. Fargo met another setback in 1872 when the Central Pacific Railway crowd won control of Wells, Fargo. He had to be content with a vice presidency, but he still held his stock and it was profitable. And he remained president of American Express.

Ever since he became express agent at Buffalo in 1843, Fargo had made his home in the bustling port city. He married a childhood sweetheart from Pompey and they had eight children.

In 1868, the same year his old partner founded his girls' college, Fargo built a fabulous mansion on Buffalo's Fargo Avenue. It had a five-story tower, a chandelier of 3,000 crystals, gold door knobs, the first elevator in the city and a life sized marble statue of Charlotte Corday, the French patriot. The three Fargo daughters gave grand balls in this gingerbread palace and Gen. Phil Sheridan was among the notables entertained there. The showplace, with its grounds, covered a city block. The house was torn down in the early 1900s.

Fargo, a staunch Unionist, paid all employes who went into the Civil War their full salaries while they were in the service. He was the wartime mayor of Buffalo from 1862 to 1866. He was elected twice, a noteworthy tribute of the community to a Democrat in wartime. Fargo made liberal gifts to churches and charity.

The last months of this vigorous individualist who had risen from boy postal circuit rider to express magnate were spent in invalidism. When he died at the age of 63, he was still president of American. He was succeeded by his younger brother, James C. Fargo, who had been trained in the business since boyhood.

The story of Wells, Fargo with all its romantic glitter went into the folklore of the nation but it was the Fargo brothers' American Express that outlived all its competitors.

THE END

A CARD OF THANKS

I am very grateful to the many who helped me gather the material for this book. Particularly I wish to acknowledge the valuable assistance given me by the Local History and Reference Divisions of the Rochester Public Library.

My thanks also go to Mrs. Marie Preston, Livingston County Historian and her assistant, Miss Ann Patchett; Clarence O. Lewis, Niagara County Historian; Wilfred J. Rauber, Dansville Town and Village Historian; Mrs. Sarah T. Ziegler, Palmyra Historian; the directors of the Wood Memorial Library and Museum in Canandaigua; the Richmond Memorial Library in Batavia and the James Prendergast Free Library in Jamestown; to Clifford A. Orr of the Public Relations Office of Hobart and William Smith Colleges at Geneva and the colleges' Librarian and to the Reference Division of the Grosvenor Library in Buffalo.

	DATE DUE		

**Member Of
Chautauqua-Cattaraugus Library System**